HERE AND THERE

The Author

1918   1968

HERE

AND

THERE

A Medley of Memories

ERNEST HAMBLOCH

JOHNSON

—

LONDON

66.728.

First Published 1968

S.B.N. 85307 014 8

PRINTED AND MADE BY CAHILL & CO. LIMITED
PARKGATE PRINTING WORKS
PARKGATE STREET, DUBLIN 8
FOR JOHNSON PUBLICATIONS.
11/14 STANHOPE MEWS WEST, LONDON S.W.7

To

"the lady constant, kind, and dear,"

My Wife

CONTENTS

CHAPTER I

CHAPTER II

CHAPTER III

CHAPTER IV

CHAPTER V

CHAPTER VI

CHAPTER VII

CHAPTER VIII

CONTENTS

Chapter 1

Quires and Places — From St Marylebone to St Paul's — Preachers and Sermons — Episcopal and Archiepiscopal — The Diamond Jubilee.

PERHAPS all choir-boys regard themselves as performers and the congregation as the audience. I know I did. We lived in London in a flat at Portman Mansions, and I went to the Marylebone parish school. I was barely seven when the headmaster, Loombe C. Brook, a formidable bearded figure invariably dressed in a black raglan cape and shiny top hat, came to our class of very small boys with the Church organist, William Hodge, and asked if any boys would like to join the choir. I at once stood up, very shy to find myself a unit of one. Hodge tried my voice, and it was news to my mother when I came home and announced with an air of some importance that I had "joined the choir." My mother took my sister and me to church on Sunday mornings, but I had always wanted to be a performer.

I think the building may have exercised a kind of histrionic influence. Architecturally at any rate, the interior of St Marylebone Church is an auditorium theatrically disposed. Externally, both this church and St Pancras Church share with the Haymarket Theatre the distinguishing feature of a Corinthian portico of six columns. Those who do not like them blame Hardwick. Those who do, praise Nash. But it is the interior of the Marylebone Church, with its flat multi-coloured ceiling and its general lay-out, which suggests a theatre. The dress circle is there; so is the typical upper circle; while the lofts flanking the choir and altar might be the boxes of a theatre. The whole is suggestive of the Georgian interior of the Theatre Royal, Bristol.

Seen from the choir, the predominant colouring of the church was the pinkish mauve wash covering the stucco cherubs that stood out in relief on the apron of the dress and upper circles. To me, as a boy of seven, it was all very gay. But what impressed me even more was the mosaic flooring of the choir. I asked my father why the little coloured stones were called mosaics. At home we were used to his jesting, so I did not take him too seriously when he said : "Named after Moses probably; but you'd better ask your choirmaster." Which I never did, for it seemed to me quite appropriate that the little coloured lozenges should be named after so very important an Old Testament figure as Moses. I used to study the patterns in order to beguile the tedium of Canon Barker's long sermons.

Canon Barker was the Rector, and his two Sunday sermons were adapted for his two congregations: abstruse and very learned for the well-to-do people who came to the 11 o'clock (comfortable hour) morning service; and for the domestic servants of these people a simpler sermon at the evening service. There was an afternoon service too, with a much rehearsed anthem.

The full choir practices of men and boys in the church on Friday evenings were conducted by Hodge, whose assistant, Frederick Kiddle, was at the organ. But we boys were trained in small classes during the week, after school, in a room over the church vestry. Hodge came from time to time; but it was Kiddle who usually took the classes. In his absence, a fair-haired boy did so. The elder boys addressed him familiarly as Leo. He was about thirteen, though he looked much older and could take the boys through a practice with the quiet assurance of a grown man. Hodge and Kiddle always seemed able to put themselves in a choir-boy's place and understand his diffi-culties. Leo, slow-spoken and aloof, appeared unable to comprehend what it was that a boy found difficult. Leopold Stokowski had passed the entrance examination of the Royal College of Music when he was only ten. William Hodge, a really good musician, gave the young man every encourage-ment.

Kiddle was already developing into a first-class piano

accompanist. An older generation of *Punch* readers may remember his name being pleasantly associated with that of an equally well-known colleague on the concert platform. There was an amusing little poem about the "inevitable" Kiddle and Liddle. The facial expression of piano players is interesting to watch. Kiddle's was remarkably like that of Claude Arrau, even to the occasionally dropped lower jaw. This was particularly noticeable in Arrau's earlier years as a performer when I heard him play in Brazil in the 1930's.

In the case of a conscientious choirmaster like Hodge no items of the choral services were too insignificant for careful practice, and it was a point of honour that the singing, once a year, of Stainer's *Crucifixion* should be as flawless as practice could make it. The work was popular with all parish choirs; but the Marylebone choir had a prescriptive right to it. On the title page of the score the composer had written: "Inscribed to his pupil and friend, W. Hodge, and the Choir of Marylebone Church."

John Stainer, whose connexion with St Paul's Cathedral was a long one as choir-boy and later as organist, may have been no musical genius; but he was a very competent musician, and he did more than any other man of his time to render church services attractive to people who might otherwise have found church-going a bore. Stainer's great achievement was to have reformed cathedral music and placed it within the reach of parish choirs and the comprehension of parish congregations.

In William Hodge's day Marylebone was an example of parish-church choir singing at its best. There was nothing slipshod in Hodge's methods at Friday evening rehearsals. Perched on a small wooden podium between the first two pews of the nave, where he could dominate choir and organ, he, the kindliest of men, would be a stern taskmaster. Sometimes there were instrumentalists for a special service. If so, they would be squeezed in between the choir and the altar. Of course, I was convinced that nobody could possibly know so much about music as Mr Hodge did.

Whenever he took after-school practice in the room over the

vestry I was fascinated, while watching his hands moving over the keyboard, to see that the tips of his fingers were turned up. Later, at St Paul's, I noticed that Sir George Martin's finger tips showed a similar upward curve, though in his case much fainter. The hands of Dr Charles Macpherson, a far more brilliant organ player than either of the other two, were quite different. They were a model of symmetry and sinewy strength.

It was in 1894 or 1895 that the Royal Choral Society under Sir Joseph Barnby gave Gounod's *Redemption* at the Albert Hall. In it are two passages to be sung by a Celestial Choir of treble voices. Hodge was the Society's organist, and about a dozen of us choir-boys from Marylebone were chosen to sing the few bars – from Heaven. We knew the oratorio from having sung it at our parish church. I found the rehearsal more exciting than the actual concert two days later, because everything was new and, looking down from our places just under the roof, I could see my mother, whom Hodge had invited to attend, in the front row. We boys, on arriving, had mounted what seemed to be endless stairs to reach the topmost gallery, where we were ranged alongside the grey chimney-like 32 ft organ pipes. Looking down to the left I could see Hodge at the organ. Immediately below were the singers, the orchestra, and the conductor. Beyond, were the vast unpeopled spaces of the auditorium. The soloist was the American-born opera singer Esther Palliser, who, I thought, looked very beautiful in her evening gown.

Kiddle was with us boys to make sure we did not miss our cue. "Behold the King of Glory! He mounts up through the sky . . . Unfold, ye portals everlasting" sang the massed chorus below in a confident C major. To which we, with becoming humility as being nearer heaven, replied in C minor: "But who is He, the King of Glory?" Sir Joseph Barnby raps with his bâton, looks up and says: "Don't be afraid to sing out." We do it again and he says: "That was much better. Sing it like that on the night."

We go downstairs again, and I am allowed to sit with my mother and stay till the end of the rehearsal. When it is over, Barnby turns to the men and says: "You must all come properly

14

attired on the night—in evening dress. As for you, ladies," he says, addressing himself to the sopranos and altos, "if you will take Miss Palliser for a model"—and he makes her a bow—"I am sure you could not do better." That was what my mother called "a really nice compliment." My father's comment when she told him was: "Evidently Sir Joseph Barnby, besides being a good musician, is a finished diplomatist. Perhaps that accounts for his having made such a success of the Royal Choral Society."

A few weeks later, came news that Hodge had died suddenly while on holiday. This upset me, for he had always been particularly kind to me. He had, for instance, taken me in his brougham to the Albert Hall on the night of the concert and brought me home again. Hodge's death made me realize for the first time that it is not only old people who die, or people like my mother's grandfather who had been killed in the Crimean War. There was a special choir practice for a memorial service for Hodge. As usual, we boys waited outside the vestry entrance of the church for Kiddle to come. Some of the boys were playing leap-frog. One of the elder boys was leaning against the door scraping a stick of Spanish with his penknife. "Fancy Mr Hodge dying!" I said. "I wonder what he died of."

The boy continued scraping his Spanish. After a pause he began chewing it. "I know what Hodge died of," he said almost contemptuously. "He wricked his guts." This rather horrified me. Not on account of the vulgar expression. There was plenty of vulgarity in the boys' talk at Marylebone School, and there was little reverence for anybody. A riddle like "Why is Queen Victoria like a flower pot?" was quite common and taken as a matter of course. But a vulgar expression applied to Mr Hodge did come as a shock. "Wricked his guts getting up from a sofa," the boy was repeating, evidently enjoying my discomfiture. "And if he had had a mercury pill handy," he added, "he'd still be alive."

I have no idea where the boy got all this from; but quite by chance I recently came across an allusion to the Bills of Mortality for the City of London in 1719. Among the causes of death were: Pain in the Head, 1; Twisting of the Guts, 54;

Rising of the Lights, 76; Lethargy, 7; Swelling in the Knee, 1; and Suddenly, 118.

* * *

The London of those days was a city of horse-drawn vehicles —buses and trams, growlers and hansom cabs—of the runaway horse and cart, of a broken-limb horse pole-axed in the street, of the swift-moving little pony and trap of the butcher's boy, a city of hawkers and crossing sweepers, of muffin men and lamplighters, of stays and bustles for the women and Hengler's circus for the children, of red-tunic soldiers wearing little pill-box headgear and ogling the nurse maids. But it was a city of few telephones, and their lack could prove awkward. My throat was persistently giving trouble, and medicines prescribed by the family physician did little good. It was decided that my father should take me to be examined by Dr Lennox-Browne, known as Dr Larynx-Browne by those who delight in such pleasantries. At Harley Street, after I had been examined, the conversation between the specialist and my father went like this:—

"I shall have to operate."

"When?"

"Now."

"Now? But I should like to consult my wife first. She decides all these things. I had better see her first and take the boy home, and—"

"Take him away! Take him away!" broke in the surgeon waving a hand impatiently. "And if the boy gets an infected throat on the way home and dies, don't blame me."

So I was operated on then and there. As there were no telephones, the first thing my mother knew about what had happened was the sight of me when, escorted by my father, I arrived home holding a slightly blood-stained handkerchief to my mouth. It was all very successful, but entailed a few weeks' convalescence.

* * *

My father was fond of banter. He had a good sense of humour, though I never heard him crack a joke. He used to delight in telling inquisitive people quite casually that the name Hambloch came from his being descended from a French Franciscan monk. In prim Victorian days the statement was calculated first to shock and then to be treated as a rather daring joke. In point of fact it was perfectly true. The naughty implication was that a French monk had broken his vow of celibacy. That was not quite exact. He had done more. He had broken with the Roman Catholic Church and adhered to the *religion réformée*. In other words he became a Huguenot. Like so many others of the same persuasion, he fled to Holland. In 1704 *le père Antoine Hambloch* published a book of prayers [*Hortulus sacrarum precationum*], a copy of which is on the shelves of the *Bibliothèque Nationale* in Paris.

My mother, née Mary Whitehouse, was born in Bristol, but like her many brothers and sisters was brought up in Bath. All the family—Whitehouses, Meads, and Cattleys—were natives of Somerset. Her diction was perfect, and the many foreigners who came to our flat, mostly business connexions of my father's, were always enthusiastic about how they could perfect their English by talking with her. Nobody ever passed a dull moment in her company, for she was a gay and amusing conversationalist with a wide range of interests, besides being a good musician.

When my father died unexpectedly at the age of forty, my mother, quite unversed in commercial affairs, soon proved herself an able business woman. She took over his factory in London and managed it single-handed at a time—the 1890's—when the mere appearance of a lady in the City was an event, and the management of a business by a woman a phenomenon.

My sister Emily Louie had a very successful scholastic career. In 1896 she gained a scholarship at the St Marylebone School. Two years later she won a County Council scholarship to the North London Collegiate School for Girls, the headmistress of which was Dr Sophie Bryant, who became a valued friend of my mother's. From there my sister went to Cambridge, having won a St Dunstan's exhibition for mathematics and been awarded, as well, the leaving school scholarship for 1903. She took a mathematical tripos at Girton and her M.A. degree at Trinity College, Dublin. After a spell at the London School of Economics and a lectureship at Portsmouth, she went to South Africa as Senior Mathematical mistress at the Pretoria High School for Girls. Later she was successively headmistress of the Girls' High Schools at Potchefstroom and Johannesburg.

She represented the Union of South Africa at the 14th International Congress of Secondary Education held in London in 1932. There she met the Roumanian delegate, Dr Wladimir Ghidionescu, Minister of Education at Bucharest. He had been a friend of mine when he was taking a post-graduate course in psychology at the Zurich Polytechnic in 1905. I shall say more of him later.

* * *

During my time at Marylebone, from 1893 to 1896, I progressed at normal speed through various "standards." There was no organized sport at the school; but we had instruction in gymnastics and wrestling.

In the teaching methods there were two key ideas: discipline and concentration. Failure in these brought with it the sanction of immediate punishment. There was plenty of caning for inattention during lessons. One master in particular had an almost diabolical competence in inflicting pain. Obviously, if you put a cane in a teacher's hand and tell him he can use it as he thinks fit, much will depend on his own temperament in administering punishment. I never knew a boy bear ill-will to a master for his caning.

After I had become a chorister at St Paul's Cathedral in 1896, it was only very rarely that I looked back on the three years I had spent at St Marylebone School. But when I did, I was astonished at the number of things I had begun to learn there: things of which it was evident to me that neither the boys nor the masters at St Paul's Cathedral Choir School had any knowledge. No doubt, there was in those days a great gulf fixed between technical schools and grammar schools. At

Choir House the grammar school tradition could be traced back to the days when a twelfth-century Bishop of London, Richard de Belmeis, the first of two of the same name, founded a school for "the Children of Paules" on the site of the school erected in Carter Lane in 1875.

Among the things I had begun to learn at Marylebone were freehand and model drawing; but the only mention ever made of drawing at Choir House was in connexion with the Woman of Samaria. I never felt that I should ever excel at drawing, whereas my sister could paint and draw really well. I did learn to write DR and CR in bold letters which I was told had to figure in ledgers, and there was line-ruling in red ink, all of which apparently had to do with the mysterious profession of book-keeping. I had begun, too, to learn the rudiments of Pitman's shorthand, and had indeed got some way beyond the PBTD stage before I left Marylebone.

Presumably there is something to be gained from learning geography by rote, and if I had stayed long enough at Marylebone I might have become a human gazetteer by virtue of the repetitive-rhythmic methods adopted there. Thus, when the teacher asked the class to name the rivers on the east coast of England we all shouted in one breath The-Humber-the-Wash-the-Mouth-of-the-Thames. Or again for the teacher to utter the word Pennine was to be answered by thirty or forty boys chanting in unison Cross Fell, Whernside, Ingleboro, Penyghant, Peak IN DERBYSHIRE. To learn, as one did, that Manchester stood on the Irwell while Ipswich did so on the Orwell was to be made conscious for life that these rivers existed. But I found "Jog" very boring until one day, probably on patriotic instructions from Whitehall, a map of West Africa was hung on the easel, instead of the usual map of England and Wales. On the new map the teacher's pointer would travel to places like Ashanti and Kumasi. Then, some time later, we were told that the war there was over and King Prempeh taken prisoner. The map was taken down. I was sorry to see it go, for Ashanti had no rivers or mountains, at least none that I had to learn by heart.

There was a chemical laboratory; but I never penetrated its

mysteries; and there was a class in carpentry in which I toiled unsuccessfully for two terms. The English lessons I liked. There were, it is true, tiresome things like grammar and parsing (incidentally, well taught), but there were compensations. I was fascinated by the visions and rhythm of "Sweet Auburn, loveliest village of the plain" when we were introduced to it. I came home full of enthusiasm, and on being asked who the teacher was replied that I thought his name was Suicide—a suggestion greeted with hilarious incredulity.

It turned out that the name was Silverside, which I personally found even funnier. He was a pupil teacher of about nineteen years of age. He wore a very high collar and had the beginnings of a moustache. He and a fellow pupil teacher would sometimes throw chalky dusters at each other, and I was appalled at the thought that the headmaster, a real martinet, might appear on the scene. If he did, I was sure something dreadful would happen to Mr Silverside, whom I liked.

In the class above, to which I was soon promoted, I was introduced to Julius Caesar, and the new master showed two of the senior boys, who declaimed quite well, how to make the most of the dramatic possibilities of the quarrel between Brutus and Cassius.

My very first introduction to St Paul's Cathedral was not when I became a chorister there. It was when I found myself standing in Canon Alley with the other choir-boys from Marylebone Church, waiting for Kiddle to give the signal for us to enter the Cathedral by the North Door. It was a dark night and the narrow passage was but feebly illuminated by a single gas lamp. I was merely aware of a massive shadow that seemed to overhang the passage in which we stood. However, when we did get in I was duly impressed. Our St Marylebone looked so small by comparison with St Paul.

The occasion was a Sons of the Clergy festival, and for some reason or other the choir of St Marylebone had been chosen to sing at an evening service in the Cathedral. It was, and perhaps still is, a tradition that the anthem to be sung at this annual service shall be the Hallelujah Chorus. I was then, in 1893, the youngest boy in the choir, and I from Decani and my

slightly older opposite number from Cantoris had to lead the
processions in and out of the service. Wherein much pride!
But my lasting impression of that evening was not the bishop
who preached, though I had never seen one before, nor the
huge congregation, but the flames from hundreds of open gas
jets placed round the dome just under the Whispering Gallery.

My poor father would have come within the Bills of Mortality
classification that I have already referred to, under the heading
Suddenly. He had been overstrained trying to straighten
things out in his business after his partner had embezzled and
decamped. But nobody had suspected that my father had a
weak heart. One day he had a cardiac seizure that was fatal.
Despite the shock, and in the midst of the turmoil of, to her,
quite strange conditions relating to industrial affairs, my
mother, who never in her life lost her head, did not on this
occasion lose her bearings. Placing all her own savings and
her husband's life insurance into the business, she saved it
from extinction, though she could not arrest its eventual
decline: it was foredoomed to be a victim of the Merger process
of Squeeze-out-the-Small-Man that was to become such an
everyday affair in the world of business after the second World
War. But my mother carried the business on long enough for
my sister and me to be educated until we could fend for
ourselves.

I was too young to appreciate the full meaning of the change
from the easier conditions of living in my father's time; but not
too young to be profoundly impressed by my mother's
unfailingly cheerful courage.

Some of my father's former friends in the City were liberal—
with advice to his widow. "You cannot reconstruct the Continental side of your husband's business. That he ran himself,"
they told her. "But the business should last some years in its
reduced form, as you are running it. What you have to do is set
your boy to work to earn his living at the earliest possible
moment."

"How old is your boy?" asked another of these City friends.
"Getting on for ten? Well, in three years' time you should
get him into some job. Education? Pooh! Look at me! I

never had any, and I'm a rich man now. Education is no good for business. Got to be hard in business. Give knocks and be prepared to take 'em. Education fills your head with a lot of rubbish that's no use to you afterwards. Put the boy to work when he's thirteen. He won't learn anything worth knowing after that. He'll only be wasting his time and your money if you keep him at school And it's money makes the world go round. These are the chaps that talk," he said, pulling a handful of sovereigns from a trouser pocket, "the Yellow Boys!"

My mother had other views and other plans. She decided that I should try for a place in the Choir School of St Paul's Cathedral. But there was an age limit, which meant that I stood only one chance and there was an examination to be passed before being admitted to a voice trial. The subjects were: "The leading incidents of Holy Writ and the Church Catechism; reading; writing; and the four elementary rules of Arithmetic."

"I think you could manage those subjects," said my mother. "But there is Latin Grammar too, and you don't know any Latin."

"No," I said dejectedly. Then, after some thought, I said brightly: "But I know *Mensa*."

"You know what?" said my mother mystified.

"I know *Mensa*, a Table," I cried triumphantly, and rattled off: "*Mensa, mensae, mensae, mensam, mensa, mensa.* That's Latin!"

The explanation was that one morning the top-hatted headmaster at Marylebone—I never saw him without the hat on his head—came into the English class where Brutus and Cassius were quarrelling. He interrupted them, and when he had cleaned the blackboard wrote on it:

Nom.
Gen.
Dat.
Acc.
Voc.
Abl.

"Now," he said, turning to the class, "you are doing Julius Caesar. Caesar was a Roman, and the Romans spoke Latin. Their language had several cases, and what I have written on the board stands for those cases. They are Nominative, Genitive, Dative, Accusative, Vocative, and Ablative." These words, in accordance with the repetitional system in force, we had to repeat out loud several times. After which the head-master said: "*Mensa* is the Latin for a Table, and so we get—" and he turned to chalk up in his best College-of-Preceptors handwriting a number of words. When he had finished the result on the blackboard was:

Nom.	*Mensa*	A Table
Gen.	*Mensae*	Of a Table
Dat.	*Mensae*	To or For a Table
Acc.	*Mensam*	A Table
Voc.	*Mensa*	O Table!
Abl.	*Mensa*	By, With or From a Table.

All of this I found utterly imcomprehensible. How could one word mean By, With, or From a Table? But what puzzled me most was that anybody, even a Roman, should ever want to say O Table! And the top-hatted headmaster never told us. That was the end of the only lesson in Latin I had ever had. I think he must have scrapped the idea of teaching any of us Latin. He went away after showing the form master a paper and saying something that sounded to me like Overcrowded Syllables.

Apparently the only master in the school who knew any Latin was Kieltie, the chemistry teacher. It was arranged that he should give me private lessons. He was a dark-haired, soft-voiced Irishman, who smelt of chemicals and tobacco. He had the reputation of being short-tempered in class; but I found him quite friendly. Incidentally, the headmaster at once lost all claim to infallibility when I found that the order of declension cases had long since become different from what he had written on the blackboard. We soon advanced beyond *Mensa* and had even begun to attack some of the outlying

23

breastworks of the formidable conjugations when I ran up against *Hic, Haec,* and *Hoc.* To me it seemed quite incredible that any people at any time in history should ever, except as a joke, have made such sounds. I laughed outright. But in obedience to Kieltie's "Don't be silly!" managed with great self-restraint to negotiate such strange sounds as *Hujus* and *Huic* without exploding. But the plural sounds were too much for me, and it took two lessons before I could meet *Hi, Hae,* or *Horum* without spluttering and incurring Kieltie's rebukes.

For the rest, I was a willing pupil and Kieltie crammed expertly, so that when in due course I and some forty other small boys presented ourselves at Choir House, I was one of the few who passed the education test and were allowed to proceed to the voice test.

At a grand piano in the big schoolroom was seated an athletic man with fair hair and a ginger moustache. He was Charles Macpherson, the sub-organist. At the master's desk in the middle of the room stood Dr George Martin, a short, much older man, very neatly dressed. As organist and choir-master he had raised the standard of singing at St Paul's to a very high level. At the boy's voice test he listened attentively, occasionally stroking his small fair beard reflectively. The test consisted of singing a few scales and attacking a few notes sounded at random on the piano. Failure to hit notes fair and square—scooping, as it is known professionally—is the defect of many professional singers and the highly paid vice of all crooners.

It was part of the duties of the head boy of the Choir School to assist the two examiners by acting as Clerk of the Court, ushering the small candidates in and out. Five years later, after I had been discharging this duty, I wrote to my mother: "As usual, one or two of the kids marched up to the piano rather cockily with 'I know that my Redeemer liveth' under one arm and 'Hear my Prayer' under the other. Also as usual they didn't get in, and of course they were not asked to sing their Pretty little Pieces for not so Pretty little Singers."

What happened was that many fond mothers were quite sure that Little Eric's precocious proficiency would melt the heart, as well as charm the ears, of the examiners. It was never put to the test. It was the quality of the voice and the ear of the boy that were tested. The training of boys' voices is a specialist's job. Faulty training can wear out a boy's voice long before its normal breaking phase. The singing of a single scale would often tell Martin and Macpherson all they wanted to know.

As I was one of four boys who had passed the test, Kiddle, who had succeeded Hodge as organist at Marylebone Church, lost no time in taking me round to Canon Barker's house presumably to receive the great man's blessing.

"So you are going to St Paul's," said the Rector genially. He had often greeted my father and me when we met in Regent's Park very early on Sunday mornings, he rehearsing, with lips moving, the sermon that he would be preaching at the 11 o'clock service. "I am a prebendary of St Paul's," he said, "so I shall see you there occasionally. And you must be sure and do us credit."

I said "Yes" dutifully; but had no idea what a prebendary was.

"Now here's a point," said Canon Barker, turning to Kiddle. "You play the organ there."

"Occasionally," replied Kiddle, "if Dr Martin and Mr Macpherson happen to be both away."

"Very well, I expect you will agree with me," said the Canon, settling himself back in his chair, "that they sing the Psalms much too fast." Kiddle made a deprecative gesture. "Yes, I know," went on the Rector, "the choir is very well trained."

"Admirably," said Kiddle, "and the results are magnificent."

"No doubt, no doubt," said the Canon impatiently. "But I wish they wouldn't sing the Psalms so fast. I can't keep up with them."

I was shocked that anybody, even a prebendary, whatever that was, should venture to criticize anything to do with St Paul's, to which I had subconsciously already transferred my allegiance.

25

"God forbid that I should glory, save in the cross of our Lord Jesus Christ." The Latin version of these words, in large letters, ran round the façade of the Choir School that was built in 1875 to house forty boy-choristers of St Paul's in Carter Lane. The text was evidently meant to serve as a reminder to successive generations of boys not to be puffed up with pride just because they happened to have good voices. All the same, we should have been strange creatures if we had not been proud to be where we were.

The school at Carter Lane has now been razed to the ground, and the new Choir School is sited, perhaps not inappropriately, midway between God and Mammon. It faces the east end of Wren's Graeco-Roman cathedral and turns its back on a red brick neo-Georgian monstrosity that houses a dependency of the Bank of England. The money-changers continue to be addicted to the forecourts of the Temples of the Lord.

Choir Schools are a peculiarly English institution. There is no lack of books on the vicissitudes of St Paul's as a building and as a *cathedra*. In some of them there are passing references to the choristers. It was not until the year 1812 that anybody paid much attention to the welfare of the boys who sang in the choir. In that year a young lady, Maria Hackett, rich and energetic, comes into the picture. Having placed a young protégé of hers in the choir, she was naturally interested in finding out how he fared there. To her horror she discovered that the boy-choristers were neglected and, under some choirmasters, actually ill treated. Maria Hackett and Florence Nightingale were "sisters under their skin." Both were tireless in bombarding high-placed Bumbledom and, in the end, defeating it. Miss Hackett actually instituted legal proceedings against the Dean and Chapter of St Paul's, after finding them quite impervious to all complaints. They were, it appears, past-masters in the art of passive resistance.

To Maria Hackett was due the movement for getting the boys better housed. From a house in Amen Court they were moved to the Chapter House in 1848. Sir John Stainer was one of the choir-boys then (1847–1856).

The kind of music that is sung in the Cathedral depends on

the whims and tastes of passing precentors, succentors, and organists. But it is all church music—from Palestrina down to the modern music makers.

Musicians have figured prominently in the ranks of the St Paul's Old Boys. So have priests. But though there have been canons and prebendaries among them, and though one of them attained the dazzling distinction of deanery, not a single bishopric has fallen to their lot. Perhaps, to judge from some modern episcopal vagaries, the St Paul's Choir School noviciate was too orthodox.

In other walks of life former St Paul's boys have done well, and some have been conspicuous: a president of the Royal College of Surgeons, senior officers in Navy, Army, Air Force and Civil Service, as well as actors, radio, and television performers. The City has absorbed many former choristers, though I know of none who has become a merchant prince.

In literature the Choir School in Carter Lane produced— one may use the word almost literally—no less a personage than Walter de la Mare. His career as poet and writer began in the boot room of the basement of Choir House. There, in the year 1889, at the age of fifteen, he and a companion, John Bouquet, who became a canon of Canterbury Cathedral, wrote and edited the first issue of a publication, *Excelsior*—the Choristers' Magazine. The early numbers were inky cyclo-styled sheets, but it was soon promoted to print. It still flourishes.

In a private letter written, only three months before his death, to Mrs Price, wife of the then (1956) headmaster of the Choir School, Walter de la Mare says: "I can recall quite clearly the hoarse whisper of the Verger who used to talk to visitors in the Whispering Gallery, and precisely the same strange, slightly ghostly sensation which mention of the Unsafe Gallery always produced in my interior. It is strange and hardly credible to recall the ecclesiastics who came to preach, including Prebendary Rowe, who, minute in stature, had the habit (fascinating to watch) of muttering; and on one sublime occasion when he came to preach his prebendarian sermon (which nicely rhymes with Mary Ann, by the way) was moved to eloquence—and to losing his balance on the stool put ready

27

for his sermon in the pulpit. The sounding board over the latter
had unusual effects on that occasion, and I can see him now,
reappearing from his temporary eclipse, without injury or even
disquietude. . . ." Walter de la Mare then goes on to recall
"that perfect sunshine of the last few days, when I *basked*—
much too certain, I think really, that I should not be trans-
mogrified into a lizard. But what a good headline in the evening
newspaper!"

Walter de la Mare mentions a prebendarian sermon! I can
vividly recall some of the many sermons I heard preached from
under the huge pulpit sounding board, and I often wondered
if it might not one day break away from its suspending chain
and snuff out the preacher. At the turn of the century the Dean
and Chapter could field a proficient team of preachers: Dean
Gregory and Canons Holland, Newbolt, Sinclair, and Winnington Ingram.

To-day relatively few members of the Church of England
seem to feel under any compulsion to attend church in order
to bear witness to the faith they profess by a public act of
corporate worship. Of course, the BBC enables people to take
their religion seated in comfort at home, and perhaps it may
soon be contrived that young people shall be confirmed by the
laying on of episcopal hands over appropriate wave lengths.
As far back as the 1890's Dr Stubbs, Bishop of Oxford, had
foreseen the possible trends of modernity and the need for
"bringing the rubric up to date." The charge to god-parents,
he suggested, should be changed so as to read: "Ye are to take
care that the Bishop be brought to this child to confirm him."

At St Paul's in my time, however, the glory was not departed
from Israel. They were the days when Canon Scott Holland
could speak of the Cathedral's "crowded glory," and Canon
Newbolt wrote of "the huge congregations which assemble at
the services on Sundays. Few clergy," he went on, "can look
unmoved from the marble pulpit at the sea of heads which
reaches right away into the nave and the transepts." Bishop
Ingram, too, in the very first sermon he preached as Canon in
Residence, in February, 1898, would be saying: "Here in St
Paul's Cathedral there fronts the pulpit a great sea of faces."

And Archbishop Lang in 1901, the year of his consecration as Bishop of Stepney, said "St Paul's was at its zenith."

One sometimes wonders whether people no longer go to listen to sermons in the Cathedral because preachers are less eloquent than they were, or whether preachers are less eloquent because people do not go there to listen to them.

Dean Gregory preached on Sunday mornings, but infrequently. His sermons were the man: downright and no words wasted. Regularly, twice a day and three times on Sunday, he would stump across to the Cathedral from the Deanery, more often than not accompanied by his wife who looked small and frail beside this burly old man verging on eighty. He had a florid complexion and a wealth of silky white hair hanging low over his neck. The policemen on point duty would hold up the horse-buses and cabs to let this venerable figure get safely across on his fat, gaitered legs.

As Canon and then Dean for over thirty years the Very Reverend Robert Gregory must have known every word of the Cathedral services by heart. But there is, it would seem, a kind of concentration which can prevent the mind from becoming stupefied by monotonous repetition. Kneeling at his stall, the old man would support his massive head on one hand, and with eyes closed follow every word of whatever prayer or collect the Minor Canon would be intoning. One became aware of his attention, because at the end of each prayer his voice would be heard. Before the choir had even begun to sing its *legato* Ah-men, the old Dean would have interposed a very audible *staccato* Eh-men.

It was Gregory who, after his appointment as Canon in Residence in 1868, bustled the whole Cathedral administration out of its old slipshod ways and made possible orderly and punctual services with an adequate attendance of clergy and choir. These business-like qualities appealed to Pierpont Morgan, and it was to the generosity of the American business magnate that the Cathedral owed its first electric lighting installation. The various experiments in chandeliers and lustres were the subject of much animated discussion among us in the Choir School.

29

Of the Chapter preachers, Canon Scott Holland was the born orator. His eloquence could be torrential, and he would go back to Amen Court completely exhausted after his Sunday sermon. In his sermons doubts and questionings, unbelief itself, were swept away into nothingness. He made the sheer beauty of Christianity shine out supreme. No written words, not even his own, can convey the effect produced by a natural orator on his hearers. But one can catch a glimpse of Scott Holland's style of oratory in a preface he wrote to some of his collected sermons. The sermons, he says, "claim to suggest a single and paramount idea; to convey a single impression; to communicate a single impulse; to verify a single supposition; to witness to a single source; to promote a single interest; to work under a single direction; to tend towards a single conclusion." Only an orator could write like that.

Canon Holland was the despair of shorthand writers, so rapid was the outpouring of words as he approached the climax of a concept. His sermons sounded extempore; but they were not. They were written. But when he came to speak, the words flowed almost spontaneously. After one of his impassioned climaxes I have seen him turn over pages and pages of his manuscript. He had not even glanced at it. In his actual hand-writing the words were shaped, not written letter by letter, for he wrote at an amazing pace. As he delivered his sermon, his reasoning was shot through with emotion. His voice rose and fell naturally, and could be tender and soft. He never shouted. But when he suddenly shot out his long surpliced arm—he was over 6 ft tall—he seemed like some mediaeval knight sending forth a mighty challenge. There were no mikes to aid the speakers in those days. But Canon Holland's voice in this challenge would ring round the dome and down the long nave. The echoes would die away, and there would be a great silence —a silence "that could be felt." Then the tension would relax, and Holland would lean down over the pulpit cushions and begin explaining so quietly and persuasively the inner meaning of his challenge and its utter irrefutability by doubters and disbelievers.

To hear Scott Holland was an exhilarating experience. To

know him was to find one's brain constantly on the alert to keep up with his lightning sallies. Sunday morning breakfasts with him at Amen Court were joyful occasions. The generous mouth in the puckered face would be frequently breaking into a smile, and the dark brown eyes could express every mood.

"Do you like the Absent-minded Beggar, sir?" I asked him one day at the beginning of the Boer War.

"It should serve its purpose, I suppose," replied Holland drily, adding: "But I think we might have expected something better from our Kipling and our Sullivan."

In this connexion one is reminded of his sermons in St Paul's warning his hearers not to be misled by the word Patriotism, which expressed something noble. The Boer War might be defended as a political necessity. But war itself was an evil thing, and when people talked about prestige it usually meant they had a bad conscience.

From an allusion by the headmaster, Minor Canon Morgan-Brown, in one of his all-too frequent homilies to us boys, usually on purity with a capital P, I had gathered that he viewed with marked disapproval the Oberammergau Passion Play. It was "presumptuous irreverence for ignorant Bavarian peasants to impersonate Our Lord Jesus Christ and the Blessed Virgin Mary." It happened that on the following day, Sunday, another boy and I were breakfasting at Canon Newbolt's. I did not tell him what our headmaster had said, but asked him if he agreed with a view I had once heard my father express, that the Oberammergau Play was something unique.

"Indeed it is," replied Newbolt. "I made a special journey to see it. The whole thing is very reverent and most impressive."

Canon Newbolt, aided by two charming daughters, was a kindly host with quite a sense of humour; but I could never forget that I was in the presence of a priest. Years after, the portrait of Savonarola by Fra Bartolommeo in the Museum of St Mark's at Venice reminded me of Newbolt: it gave the impression of unstudied humility coupled with stern piety. For both men, the dominating thought in their teaching seems to have been: "Ye cannot serve God and mammon."

Savonarola might have died quietly in his bed if he had

31

preached to the text of The Value of Florentine Banking to the Christianity of the Renaissance, and Newbolt might have become an archbishop if he had preached on the Importance of Capitalism in the modern Christian State. Instead, he solemnly warned that "the love of money is the root of all evil." I remember well the dramatic *crescendo* of his voice when in one of his sermons Newbolt warned "this great and rich City of London" not to be like the Jewish money-changers of old, who, at a time of mortal peril to their Race and to the holy city of Jerusalem, turned a deaf ear to warnings and, gripping their money bags, muttered: "What care we? Perish the city of the Lord Jehovah!"

It is impossible to convey the contempt that Canon Newbolt put into those words. He rarely used a gesture; but this time I saw him clutching his manuscript as though he were gripping a bag of money, so that he had to smooth out his notes before going on with the rest of his sermon. If one closed one's eyes, one would never have guessed that he was reading from his notes. To the listener his sermons were an intellectual exercise.

Archdeacon Sinclair's sermons were read with great deliberation from a manuscript placed on a miniature mountain of cushions on the rim of the pulpit. There was a kind of anonymity about his sermons, because they were largely made up of long quotations from the Early Fathers, of whose existence I was first made aware by hearing the Archdeacon quote from them so often and at such length.

William Sinclair was a massive figure, immensely broad. His full-featured face had a severe cast, as of a leader who in The Forty-Five could have quelled a mutiny of undisciplined clansmen with a mere look. But he was a genial host at his Sunday morning breakfasts at the Chapter House. We went two at a time to these canonical meals, and they were much prized invitations. Sinclair's breakfasts were better weighted for boys' appetites than those of the other canons: plenty of eggs, bacon, and sausages. Paintings of his warrior ancestors hung on the walls, and he was pleased if one questioned him about them. He would relate some historical anecdote and appeal for confirmation or correction to his sister—"Janet, you can bear me out, I think"—who presided at the other end of the table. Service on Sunday mornings during his month in residence was a trial. Sinclair had a booming baritone voice and liked using it. He insisted on taking the sung Communion Service, a duty falling normally to one of the Minor Canons. The trouble was that he could not intone in tune.

I doubt if any bishop of the Church of England was ever so popular as Winnington Ingram was when he was consecrated Bishop of Stepney and became automatically a Canon Residentiary of St Paul's. People do not take camp stools and queue for long hours outside a church to hear a man preach, unless there is something magnetic in the preacher. Yet Ingram was no orator. He spoke from the briefest of notes. His power lay in re-creating an atmosphere by using anecdote. In print, a story of his that gripped his hearers is bald, even banal. I have some of his sermons, which he inscribed and gave me. Read objectively, they are poor stuff. But in reading them, one who heard them preached can hear him again and feel the undefinable influence that he exercised over his hearers.

In private life and conversation never was there a naturally more optimistic person. His vitality was amazing. With us boys he was always jolly.

Ingram's successor at Stepney was Cosmo Gordon Lang when Ingram was translated to London. Lang was quite different: pleasant, but formal and condescending. After his first Sunday afternoon sermon as Canon in Residence it was my duty as head boy to go to Amen Court to present the "respectful compliments" of the boys at Choir House. There was a crowd of visitors. Lang was in the centre of the drawing room, grasping the lapels of his coat in his habitual manner and listening while a gushing female pointed to the wall paper, which was of a bright canary yellow.

"What a perfectly ghastly wall paper!" she exclaimed in a loud voice. "What awful taste your predecessor must have had! How will you ever bear to live with it?"

"I agree it is rather horrible," said Bishop Lang. "I shall have it changed. I shall send to Scotland for specimens of some

33

c

of my favourite heathers. Then I shall get some firm here to make me a wall paper that combines all the heather colours."

To the compliments that I duly presented he replied that he hoped to see some of us at tea from time to time. After which, he turned to his adult visitors. I had been struck with the new Canon's fine voice, and admired his elocution in his subsequent sermons; but their content never stuck in my memory. Some months afterwards when my time was drawing near for leaving the Choir School, I paid the customary round of good-bye visits at Amen Court. Bishop Lang asked me what I had been reading lately. Strict adherence to truth would have required me to say that I had just finished another of Mrs Henry Wood's novels. But I felt sure this would have been frowned on. The English master had given me a small selection of Browning's poems which I read at odd moments. So I replied that I had been reading some Browning.

"Browning at your age?" exclaimed Bishop Lang. I said the master had told me they were the easier poems.

"Splendid!" said the Bishop. "Now you must have a complete edition. I will give you one. Meanwhile, here is a little book that it will do you good to read. It is the story of a very fine character: a young man I knew well, who died a short time ago on the threshold of what promised to be an exceptionally full and useful life dedicated to God." I was beginning to feel uncomfortable. It sounded like the beginning of one of the headmaster's awful pi-jaws. But I was spared. The Bishop was writing on the fly leaf: *Ernest Hambloch, from C. G. Stepney. S. Paul's. Oct.* 1901.

I did read the book, and it did not do me any good at all. Nor did I ever get the Browning the Bishop had promised me.

Dr Frederick Temple, Archbishop of Canterbury, came in state to St Paul's eight times during my last year there. That meant that each time, as head boy, I had the duty of going to the West Door to await his arrival and carry his train up the nave to his seat in the choir stalls. Similarly on various occasions when he moved to and from pulpit or altar. At the back and in the dead centre of the hem of the Archbishop's long black satin chimere was a loop. This he wore over his left wrist. The train was thus draped up and hung at his left side without touching the ground or impeding the movements of his left arm.

Dr Temple's rugged face would have been rather forbidding but for the kindly eyes. I got quite accustomed to taking the loop from him or handing it to him, having always taken the precaution of studying beforehand whatever the particular Order of Service might be. The archiepiscopal fee for this coveted job was half-a-crown.

The ritual of the tip took two forms. The Archbishop disrobed in the Dean's vestry. This is reached by a rather steep flight of steps from a door in the South choir-aisle of the Cathedral. On arriving at the vestry at the top of the stairs I would hand the loop of the train to the Archbishop and make a discreet half-turn to descend the steps, as though tips had never been known to exist. Whereupon Dr Temple would say in his rasping voice: "Wait!" and then turn to his chaplain, whose duty it apparently was to produce a half-crown piece. If he did so, the Archbishop would take it from him and hand it to me with a smile. I would say: "Thank you, sir," feigning surprise, and hurry joyfully to the Boys' vestry in the North choir-aisle. I always promised myself that I would remember to say "Your Grace" instead of "Sir," but when the occasion arose I forgot.

The other form of ritual in the matter of the tip was thus:— As often as not, when Dr Temple turned to his chaplain for the coin, that thoughtless or perhaps impecunious cleric would assume the air of Simple Simon and murmur: "Sir, I have not any" or words to that effect. The first time this happened I wondered "What now?" and was relieved to see the Archbishop turn to another quarter.

"Holland," he would say in his trailing, slightly nasal voice, "lend me half-a-crown."

Canon Holland, who did everything quickly, was by this time divested of his canonicals and was in shirt sleeves. He would put his hand in a trouser pocket, grin, and produce the coin. This Dr Temple would take and pass on to me, with his usual kindly smile. I supposed Holland would get his half-crown back. That, no doubt, was the chaplain's job.

Only one thing troubled me in the business of train-bearer. At that time Dr Temple was some eighty years old; his sight was not good, and he was naturally tired at the end of a long Service at which he had officiated, consecrated, or preached. Slowly mounting the steep steps of the Dean's vestry he would lean rather heavily on a wall banister, his body bent forward, so that the front of his rochette would sweep the step immediately above his next foot-tread. I used to keep close behind the Archbishop, holding the train of the chimere high and free, but always afraid that the old man would step on his rochette and stumble. That is precisely what happened one day. It was on one of the lower steps, and his chaplain, on his left, made a quick move towards him with outstretched arm. But Dr Temple, who had instantly recovered his balance, waved him aside, saying: "Thank you, I don't want yer help." He had nearly reached the top of the stairs when he stumbled again. The same would-be helping arm of the chaplain was officiously extended. Again it was waved aside; but this time with a rasping "Thank you, I told you I didn't want yer help." The reproof conveyed in the "I told you" was devastating.

There was no lack of Special Services outside the normal Cathedral routine, sometimes with orchestras. Of the instrumentalists two men stood out. One was Henderson, drummer of the Queen's Hall orchestra; the other was Solomon, the famous trumpet player. The orchestras were placed on some occasions between Decani and Cantoris, and it was then fascinating to watch Henderson at work surrounded by his timpani, while to listen to Solomon producing the purest of pure melodies out of a six-foot long trumpet pointed dome-wards was thrilling.

There were funeral services for artists like Millais, enthronements of bishops like Mandell Creighton, and memorial services during the Boer War. Incidentally, it was Creighton, not Lang as is sometimes thought, who was the first bishop of the Church of England since the Reformation to wear a mitre in St Paul's Cathedral. He is the only ecclesiastic I have ever seen who looked as though he was meant to wear one. The others look as though they have stolen the headgear of the Nizam of Hyderabad and are not sure how to wear it.

Stiff, beautifully embroidered but ungainly copes came into fashion while I was at St Paul's. I have heard Canon Scott Holland, who hated them, say that he and his brethren looked a collection of armadillos in them.

The great event of those years was the Diamond Jubilee of Queen Victoria, in 1897, when the St Paul's Choir led the other choirs and bands massed on the West Front steps of the Cathedral in singing "the unrivalled *Te Deum* in A" composed for the occasion by Sir George Martin.

There was plenty of excitement, more so during the rehearsals than on the actual day, because it was quite a mix-up before all the performers and others could be got into their allotted places. At the dress rehearsal I found myself next to an immensely broad-chested, weather-beaten old Russian officer much bemedalled. He wore a light blue uniform and the glossiest black top boots I had ever seen. He told me about battles at places like Plevna and Sebastopol, and when I asked him: "Who were the bravest soldiers you ever fought against?" he replied without a moment's hesitation: "The Turks."

Tuesday, June 22, 1897, was a cloudless day of brilliant sunshine. The windows and roofs of all the warehouses in the Churchyard were crowded with spectators, and there were flags and bunting everywhere. Stretched across two sides of Ludgate Hill—surely the crookedest approach in the world to a national basilica—was a broad red streamer bearing what seemed like a bad joke from the ghetto in white printed capital letters:

We are a happy family
VR   VR   VR

The arrival of the procession up Ludgate Hill led by Captain Ames—"the tallest man in the British Army"—was perfectly timed, and the singing and trumpeting on the steps of the Cathedral lasted exactly the scheduled twenty-two minutes. The royal carriage, drawn up at the bottom of the West Front steps, was no gilt coach affair, but a simple barouche type vehicle in which sat a little old lady, wearing a poke bonnet with a touch of mauve ribbon. She held an open parasol.

When the Service was over there was a bustle of bowings by the prelates nearest the royal carriage. Martin, too, went down from his high rostrum to make his bow, and we were then brought down the steps and presented to the Queen. I was surprised that the rather heavy-featured, podgy lady could smile so graciously. Then the Archbishop, breaking all the protocol arrangements, called for three cheers for the Queen. The royal carriage rolled away, so did the "captains and the kings." The curtain came down on a dying era. The 20th century of disillusions and dethronements had already begun on that sunny day in June, 1897.

Chapter II

Mrs Carr Shaw and G.B.S. — Oscar Wilde — Theatres — The ex-Governor and the Bath chair.

MY SISTER could equally well have made her career in music as in mathematics, for she was a brilliant pianist and studied singing under several competent teachers. Among them was Mrs Carr Shaw, mother of Bernard Shaw.

Shaw has told his fans how he came to London as a young man in order to throw his mother into his struggle for life. At least *her* struggle was unselfish. She used to teach singing at the North London Collegiate School for Girls where my sister was a pupil. Dr Sophie Bryant, the headmistress, had many Irish friends and thus became acquainted with Mrs Carr Shaw.

The Shaw establishment in Ireland must have been a peculiar one. An Italian was one of Mrs Shaw's lodgers there. He had some special method for good voice production and Mrs Shaw seems to have adopted it.

My sister, while at the North London School, took private lessons from Mrs Carr Shaw who was at that time living in a typical Victorian-cum-Georgian terrace house in Fitzroy Square. Mrs Shaw, whom my sister described as "very kind and very thorough," wanted her to take a solo part in some cantata she was preparing for performance on prize day at the school. The tuition my sister received was based on the system invented by the Shaws' Italian lodger in Ireland. In the house in Fitzroy Square there was a large drawing-room on the first floor with an extension over the entrance hall. In the extension stood the grand piano. There was a further extension at the back, separated from the big room by a screen with a door in

39

it and known as the back drawing-room. It was furnished
with an oval table and chairs, and after the singing lesson,
wrote my sister, Mrs Carr Shaw would ring the bell and a little
maid in cap and muslin apron would appear with a silver tray
and tea things. Tea was then taken in the back drawing-room
and Mrs Shaw would pour out tea for her pupil and herself.

"I used to love these sessions," writes my sister, "because
Mrs Shaw was always so interesting about things musical.
But sometimes, to my chagrin, 'Mr Bernard' would be
announced and he would join us at tea. I *hated* him! He would
tease his mother, contradict her, and argue about operas (of
which I was then quite ignorant). His attitude was not the
respectful one that I thought fitting for a son towards his
mother. At that time, though I did not know it, he must
already have been married; but I believe that before then he
was living on his mother, for by then she would have had a
fairly wide professional connexion. I remember that on the
occasions when he came to tea I would exclaim to mother when
I got home: 'That *awful* son of Mrs Carr Shaw's came to tea
again to-day!' No doubt, I should have done well to memorize
every single word he said.

"I have seen it alleged that Mrs Carr Shaw was 'slatternly'.
I should not have said so when I knew her. One had trained
maids in those days when one could afford them, and at Fitzroy
Square I remember no dust or untidiness. The silver on the
tea tray was always highly polished. Mrs Carr Shaw usually
wore voluminous black, which was suitable to her age and
period. . . . It is certain that Shaw's mother kept him supplied
with funds until he had established himself, and married."

My sister's notes refer to the Spring and Summer of 1903,
just before she went to Girton. She reiterates in another letter
how rude Bernard Shaw was to his mother. No doubt, Shaw's
wife did discover dust and disorder in the upstairs room at his
mother's house in Fitzroy Square occupied by him. But that
was simply because nobody was allowed to touch his papers,
and because he had a habit of cooking meals for himself and
leaving the débris all over the place. "I had no thought of
anything else but the breathing exercises and the actual

singing practice," wrote my sister; "and I looked forward to the tea with Mrs Carr Shaw afterwards, when she would tell me all sorts of things about opera and so on. The service of the neat maid she then employed was what one expected, and these sessions were spoilt for me only when the maid would appear with the news that G.B.S. was coming up for tea!"

My mother's family at Bath knew James Robinson Planché, the dramatist who, like my father, was of Huguenot origin. He was then Somerset Herald. When my mother was about seventeen, she used often to be invited to visit Planché and his daughter who were both very fond of her. He used to tell her stories that she found fascinating about the duties and functions of heralds and would show her his uniform. He was an excellent raconteur, and my mother often said that she had learnt more from the historical stories he used to tell her than she had ever learnt from history books. When my mother went to live in London, Planché's daughter gave her introductions to a distinguished Jewish family there. In the family there were several daughters, all of them talented. Their mother was a brilliant pianist. She was a daughter of Sir John Simon, who had taken an active part in the government of Jamaica and was M.P. for Dewsbury for twenty years. He was an amateur pianist and his daughter's house in London was much frequented by musicians, as well as other interesting people in artistic and literary circles. Tosti, for instance, then at the height of his popularity, came both as a friend and to teach singing to her daughters. One of them had married Ernest Leverson, a business friend of my father's.

I remember my mother relating a chance visit she had paid to Mrs Leverson and telling my father how she had "found Ada closeted with a strange man in her drawing-room." There were the usual introductions. At the moment my mother did not quite catch the name, but, she said, "I shall never forget the revulsion I felt at the man's appearance—his fleshy lower jaw, the sensuous lips, the long untidy hair and, most of all, the flabby handshake." On her way home she caught up with the name: it was Oscar Wilde. This would be about the time when the poor man's troubles were just beginning.

My mother was an enthusiastic theatre-goer. She thought it would be part of my education to have seen some of the older generation of actors. Toole I saw only as he was wheeled along in his invalid chair on the Brighton parade: but I gazed with respect. John Hare I saw in "A Pair of Spectacles," but no doubt quite rightly I was not allowed to see him in "The Gay Lord Quex." I saw Irving in "Waterloo" a year before he died. Of this play I remember two lines. One is when he cannot understand why his grand-daughter's soldier-lover does not wear a stock. He shakes his head and remains unconvinced by their explanations about modern uniform. "The Dook would have a word to say about that," he mutters.

The other line I remember was the moment when, his mind wandering, the old soldier re-lives and recounts his part in the battle of Waterloo. He rises suddenly from his chair, faces the audience and cries out: "The Guards need powder, and by God they shall have it!" Then he sinks back into his chair exhausted —a shrivelled old man. Melodramatic, no doubt. But how effective!

In the same performance "The Bells" was given. In this piece Irving's acting did not impress me as I would have liked it to. He entered a hut when a snow-storm was raging, wearing what looked to me like patent leather shoes that had not a flake of snow on them. The author's stage direction says that Mathias "should be wearing gaiters and spurs, and a long cloak covered with snow."

When my mother was a widow we often went to stay in Brighton for the summer holidays. Our visits usually coincided with those of Sir George Couper, his wife, and two unmarried daughters. They were great friends of my mother's and sister's. Sir George Couper had had a very distinguished career in India. He had served through the Mutiny years and ended by being Governor of the North-West Provinces. His father had been Comptroller to the Household of the Duchess of Kent, Queen Victoria's mother. Lady Couper, to whom he was devoted, was an invalid.

Like many other sea-side resorts at that time, Brighton had quite a display of Bath chairs and Bath chairmen to pull or push them and their invalid occupants along the front—at a snail's pace. The Coupers did not need to hire a chair: they brought their own with them from their home in Camberley. Sir George used to pull it along the front at a great pace, so that his wife got the air and he got the exercise. He was then in his 70's—an active, wiry man, not more than 5 ft 3 in. in height. There was a tremendous "something" about the little man. He had the upright bearing of a soldier and a soldier's son. Yet, wearing his little bowler hat and a nondescript suit, he had nothing to distinguish him outwardly from the Bath chairmen. To more discerning observers there was something striking in the head-up forward-march bearing of Sir George Couper. However, the aura of pomp and circumstance of an ex-Governor from India was certainly absent as, with hands behind his back gripping the handle bar of the long shaft at the front of the Bath chair, he trailed Lady Couper after him.

There was always a small camp stool in the chair, and when Sir George was tired he would pull it out and sit down to rest alongside his wife. Sometimes they would sit near the bandstand to listen to the music. Crowds of people would be standing, because the chairs and benches round the bandstand were strongly occupied by early comers. On one occasion Sir George was seated on his camp stool when he felt a tap on his shoulder. He turned round and saw a lady standing behind him.

"My good man," she said, "I should like that stool you're using. Here's tuppence."

With a courtly bow, Sir George yielded his seat to the lady. And took the proffered two pence.

There was naturally much mirth when Sir George and Lady Couper told the story at lunch. Equally naturally, there was much discussion as to the ethics of his having accepted the lady's "tuppence". Sir George maintained that it was the only thing to do in order to save the lady from embarrassment, had she known who he was. Besides, he said, a long explanation would have disturbed the people near them who wanted to listen to the music.

"She made two mistakes," said Sir George. "One of them I quite understand. She took me for a Bath chairman. The other mistake was that she thought the camp stool was one of those belonging to the Brighton Corporation and not mine. Now all is well, and the lady is no doubt having her lunch quite happily, as we are."

"But I am still not sure that you did right in taking the 'tuppence'," said Maude, the younger Miss Couper, with a smile. "I shall have to ask Tonman."

Tonman was a furry little toy monkey belonging to Maude Couper. He sat on a console-table in the corner of her room. She used to write short stories for magazines. It would—that was the convention—have been unbecoming for the daughter of a distinguished public servant to do so, and so they were written by Tonman. If a story of hers had been rejected by an editor, Tonman was stood in the corner. If on entering Miss Couper's little sanctum you found Tonman standing on the console-table with his face to the wall, you knew that Miss Couper had just received a reject-slip from an unappreciative editor.

Chapter III

*Sutton Valence — King Jerome's Bath — The Hercules Statue —
The German Turk — From Frankfurt to Zurich — A multi-national
Pension — A downward slope.*

ON LEAVING St Paul's I went to Sutton Valence School.
They were happy years. It is true that the sudden
transition from head boy of a choir School to the Upper
Fifth of a public School was at first painfully abrupt. It was a
question of age: one had not been through the Lower School.
However the process of adaptation did not take longer than one
term. I could have gone to St Paul's, Hammersmith; but I
longed for the country. Surrounded by farms and hopfields,
Sutton Valence was far removed from urban stuffiness. I found
there was a very strong Rugger tradition in the school, so
much so that only the captain of the XV could be head boy.
Hunt and Rowlands played for Kent while still schoolboys,
and T. G. Pitt, a contemporary of mine, was in the Cambridge
XV.

At St Paul's constantly recurring special services made one
feel one was at the centre of national events; but in the quiet
countryside of Sutton Valence I felt as if I was looking at
national events through the wrong end of a telescope.

When the Boers sued for peace the event seemed a very
distant one to me. But there was a whole holiday and the head
boy marshalled us in force to go round the countryside
collecting money for fireworks and a bonfire. One of the people
whose grounds we invaded was John Corlett, founding
proprietor and editor of the *Sporting Times*. His son, an Old
Suttonian, had been killed in the Boer War. Corlett came to
the door, waved pleasantly to us, and gave the head boy some
money. I told some of the boys near me that I thought the

45

whole procedure of begging for money was wrong and humiliating. As a new boy, I was promptly squashed.

"The Pink 'Un" in those days was not *The Financial Times* as it is to-day. The name was given to Corlett's paper not only, I imagine, because of the colour of the paper on which it was printed, but because one or two of its columns contained specially collected stories calculated to bring a blush to the cheek of some of the less hardened sinners who read it. My headmaster, George Bennett, a wonderful scholar and a keen horse-rider, told me once when I was head boy how astonished he was that a really cultivated man like John Corlett could own and edit a paper like "The Pink 'Un."

"I told Corlett so", he said, "the last time I dined at his house."

"What did he say?" I asked.

"Oh, he just shrugged the matter off. Said the readers of the paper, especially those on the Stock Exchange, expected a ration of suggestive stories, and that he personally did not concern himself with that particular column. It is perhaps remarkable," went on Bennett, "that Corlett himself should be the decent fellow he is. He tells me he had no proper education at all. His father, who was a sergeant-major in the Dragoon Guards, taught him all he knows."

Corlett certainly made his way in journalism, and was president of the Press Club in 1898.

Another national event aroused some interest, at least in the VIth form, and that was in 1903 when Joseph Chamberlain, on returning from a visit to South Africa, launched his proposals for an Imperial Preferential Tariff. Bennett had the knack of interesting his VIth form in current affairs as well as in the classics, so that we were abreast of this particular question. But *The Times* sent some of us to our dictionaries when it headlined an article: "Mr Chamberlain's Fiscal Policy." After all, *fiscus* had nothing to do, at least directly, with tariffs or Customs dues.

Latin, Greek, French, German, and History were well taught at Sutton Valence. Perhaps Geography and Mathematics were too; but on them I can pass no opinion, for I was an unwilling pupil, though later in life I contrived to pass exams in both subjects. Chemistry was a closed book to me, and still remains so. At Sutton Valence most of us were "classical" and chemistry was just "Stinks".

I found three ex-choir boys at the school, besides myself: from King's College, Cambridge; and from New College and Christ Church, Oxford. So I started a male-voice quartet party, with the chaplain, who had a good tenor voice, as spare man. We had, as well, a really brilliant boy pianist, R. M. ff. Richardson, who became a professional musician, so we were well provided for in our School concerts. Our music master, Dr Henniker, sometimes let Richardson and me play in his orchestra at Maidstone. When I say "his orchestra" I mean the one he conducted. He pointed out to me one day, when there were some absentees at rehearsal and the rehearsal had gone badly, that it was not within his power to do more than protest mildly if a member of the orchestra did not turn up at rehearsal.

The Queen's Hall orchestra under Henry Wood was then in its heyday. "How does Henry Wood manage to get such a disciplined orchestra?" I asked Henniker.

"The reason is simple," replied Henniker. "Wood is a partner with Newman. That means he owns the orchestra. He can not only reprimand, but dismiss. It is when a conductor has the power of dismissal that he can really command."

I had seen Beerbohm Tree's productions of *Twelfth Night* and *Julius Caesar*. Greatly daring, I produced *Henry IV*, First Part, having persuaded Dr Henniker to write some incidental music. I enjoyed being what was then known as Acting Manager, not Producer.

All good things come to an end, however; and on my headmaster's advice I did not take two scholarships to Cambridge, as I could have done; but decided to go looking for a job on the Continent. I thought I could live at the university on £120 a year, which the scholarships would have given me. Bennett was quite sure I couldn't do it under £200. "And where are the missing £80 a year to come from?" said Bennett. To that I had no answer. Besides, my duty was to begin earning my own living without any delay.

47

Bennett held out great hopes. One of his acquaintances in the neighbouring country houses like Linton Park and The Mote was a London banker, Lehnmann, who had told him he had to employ foreigners in his bank because young Englishmen knew no languages.

"If you can come back in three years' time with fluent French and German," Bennett told me, "Lehnmann will take you on and your future should be assured."

I was grateful and assented, but confess that instinctively I never saw myself in the role of a City man. In the meantime the prospect of living abroad appealed to me. A few days later I ceased to be a schoolboy, and on a bitterly cold night in January, 1905, found myself on a steamer bound for the Hook of Holland.

My destination was Dortmund and my companion in an over-heated German railway carriage next morning was a pale man. He was reading an English periodical and was evidently disinclined for conversation. Hot coffee and rolls brought to the carriage by the attendant were welcome. My fellow-traveller had ordered a boiled egg. He left it untouched after two mouthfuls. When the attendant came back later to collect the empty trays he pointed to the egg and said: "*Das Ei war schlecht.*" I had my doubts whether that was the right way of saying that the egg was bad, and as he did not say anything more when the attendant made some perfunctory apology I concluded that he was perhaps not really fluent in German. But how much I admired the easy way in which he had uttered a simple phrase! I knew that in similar circumstances I should have been stumped and not even got the gender of egg right perhaps. I decided that there was a gap to be filled between classical and colloquial German. Experience has taught me that one doesn't really know a foreign language until one thinks in it. Translation is something quite different.

My only reason for going to Dortmund was to present a letter of recommendation given to me in London by a former business friend of my father's. It was the only recommendation I had. When I got to Dortmund I found that the man I was supposed to see was travelling. However, he knew I was

coming and had left word that I should find him at Arnsberg.
So to Arnsberg I duly went, only to find he had by this time
gone elsewhere but would communicate with me. I stayed at
Arnsberg for a couple of days. It was a little town of under
10,000 inhabitants. It is delightfully situated on the Ruhr.
Everything was neat, tidy, and sleepy. It was, I discovered, the
administrative capital of Westphalia and the chief industry
was bureaucracy. In obedience to a message from the elusive
German business man, I went to seek him out at Hamm. Herr
Dietrich was helpful, if formal. He met me at the station and
told me we should be taking an electric tram to the suburb of
Bad-Hamm.

"What do I do with my portmanteau?" I asked him.

"The tram will take it," he replied. It was my first experience
of a conductorless tram.

"Leave your portmanteau here at the corner of the street,"
said my new friend when we got out. "I will send someone to
fetch it."

Modest though my one piece of luggage was, it contained all
my worldly goods. So I asked: "Will it be all right there?"

"Of course," replied Herr Dietrich, and I felt my question
had perhaps not been tactful. It was not a busy street, but there
were plenty of passers-by, and I had hitherto had no experience
of leaving a parcel or anything else "unattended" at the corner
of a frequented street in a town of 30,000 inhabitants, and
expecting that no one would steal it, or even touch it.

Our destination was a modest house, where an old peasant
couple would put me up for a night or two. Dietrich, a bachelor,
had rooms in a near-by house. We sat and talked English-
German for quite some time before I mustered courage to ask
him: "What about my portmanteau?"

"Ah yes," he said, quite unconcerned. "I will have it
fetched." He called my new peasant-host, and I confess I was
quite relieved when he came back with it.

Dietrich was an engineer and did much travelling. He left
me in the care of the peasant couple, promising to return and
fetch me for an evening meal at a local café. In my halting
conversation with them I found myself filling up a blank for a

49

German word that escaped me with an English word. Where-upon, as often as not, the couple would signify with emphatic *Ja Ja*'s that they had understood. I then discovered that they talked *Plattdeutsch* (Low German) to each other; and so we had an amusing half-hour swapping words that were cousins or identical in Low German and English.

On my first visit, that evening, to a German café I was instructed as to the privileged place occupied by the *Stammtisch* in the hierarchy of café tables in Germany. But what impressed me most was the ritual observed by those entering a café for refreshment in winter. There was nothing casual about it: no suspicion of having a quick one. The change from the raw cold of a January winter outside was abrupt in the extreme. The atmosphere inside was stiflingly hot and smoke-laden. With great deliberation Dietrich eased off his galoshes and slid them under a circular coat-and-umbrella stand. Then he took off coat, muffler, and hat and hung them up in company with many others. I imitated him, except that I had no galoshes. Then he walked to a rack on which were hung by a ring in their wicker frames—a capital device—half-a-dozen of the score of newspapers that other customers had carried to their tables. After a quick look he suggested I study the *Frankfurter Zeitung*, which I did after we had a meal. It was my initiation to using a café on the Continent as a reading-room.

At the Hamm railway station I had been struck by the number, as well as the immense size, of the ground-level platforms.

"Why does a small town like Hamm need so many railway lines and such large platforms?" I enquired of Dietrich two days later, when he was seeing me off to a new destination.

"For troop movements, of course," he replied in the tone of one answering a rather silly question. It is true that Hamm was an important railway junction; but I had not then, in 1905, learnt to associate railway junctions with troop movements.

My new destination was Cassel, and there, on the recom-mendation of my friend Dietrich, I found myself installed as a paying guest with a German family that spoke no English.

Mr and Mrs Schmidt were a very pleasant middle-aged couple, he being an engineer friend of Dietrich.

Cassel owed much to the French Protestants to whom it opened its gates on the revocation of the Edict of Nantes. The influence seemed still to exist in many ways, owing no doubt to the work done by the administrators whom Napoleon sent to organize the Kingdom of Westphalia for his brother Jerome. It certainly owed nothing to Jerome, among whose more stupid extravagances was a marble pavilion with enormous pipes leading from a wine cellar. Here, the guide assured one, Jerome bathed in wine. I managed to ask if there was any water laid on. The answer was "in the negative."

Besides the many other objects of interest in the town, there was the Wilhelmshöhe with its artificial waterfall to be climbed. Why the whole structure should be surmounted by a copy of the Farnese Hercules, 30 ft high, nobody could tell me. But I did find out that in popular parlance the Hercules statue was known as Big Christopher, though, once again, nobody could tell me why. The "Wilhelm" who built the affair was not Kaiser Bill, but the Landgrave No. One of that name.

One wonders what *Napoléon le Petit* thought about when he was housed in the Octagon overlooking the waterfall, after Sedan. Of the hash his ambition had made of things in France? Probably not. Of his great namesake? Possibly. Of Bismarck? Often, no doubt. Of himself? Always. Used by Cavour. Crushed by Bismarck. A curious destiny.

After spending a few weeks at Cassel I risked a journey to Frankfurt in answer to an advertisement I had seen in the *Frankfurter Zeitung*, and a few days later found myself engaged as book-keeper in the office of a printing works there—Jean Rohm. My only experience was to have picked up some rudimentary knowledge by occasionally, on my holidays from school, studying the mysteries of the ledgers in our London factory.

I found the daily routine of my office job extremely boring, but I was earning and learning; and Frankfurt-am-Main had many compensations to offer. There was the Opera House, where the Heldentenor was Forchammer, who, I was told, had been the first man to sing the part of Parsifal, apart from the Bayreuth production in 1882. He had, they said, sung it in Holland, because clerical difficulties had been put in the way of producing the opera in Germany, except at Bayreuth. Forchammer had a good voice, but was an even better actor. I have never seen an Othello so powerfully acted as his, in Verdi's opera of that name. Inevitably, however, I became a Wagner fan. Pit and gallery prices were extraordinarily cheap, and that was an important consideration. I managed to see two of Schiller's plays, but the production of *Maria Stuart* was spoiled for me, because the kilts worn by the men came down so low that they looked almost like skirts.

I lived in a pension in the Rossmarkt—the site of the old horse market. It had some fine buildings and a plaque in one of them told the passer-by that in a house on that site the Rothschild family had started their banking business. The pension was run by a widow with two grown-up daughters. One of them had married an opera singer. He had given up the stage to devote his time to perfecting a railway automatic braking system. The invention, he was confident, would bring him and his wife a fortune. They were a very devoted and gay couple, in the thirties. He was always surrounded with plans and blueprints. It was evident that there was a large dose of Micawber in his composition.

One of the pensionnaires was a talented pianist; she was very shy but could be persuaded to play for us. There were half-a-dozen business men, some with wives, and there were two French young men sent by their fathers to work as *volontaires* in order to learn German. They never could manage the German aspirate. They were polite and generally liked. Indeed the whole atmosphere of the pension was very friendly. A very spruce little man, Max Rosenthal, was so obviously a German and a Jew that I was much amused that he should insist, and insist very strongly, that he was a Turk. We became good friends, and when I pressed him about his Turkish nationality he told me he had been born in Constantinople.

It was at this German pension that I first realized that an habitual cigar-smoker could be a woman. The smoker was a handsome middle-aged actress. Later, at Zurich, I met a lady who smoked her cigar just as naturally.

There were plenty of things to see and excursions to take on Sundays. I had insisted, even though I feared to offend, that I should not look in at the office on Sunday mornings. On one memorable occasion my friend Rosenthal and I went to Wiesbaden and nearly lost the last train back to Frankfurt because I was loath to leave the theatre before the very end of the last act of *Lohengrin*, which I was seeing for the first time.

Three months later, excursions and opera-going were to cease. I heard from a school friend of mine in Zurich that the British Consul there was looking for a secretary. He had mentioned me to the Consul and recommended me to apply for the job. There was, however, one condition: the applicant must know shorthand.

"I don't know how you feel about that," he wrote, "because we certainly learnt none at Sutton Valence."

What I did feel was that I must try for the job. I could see no future in the Frankfurt office, which, in any case, I cordially disliked. Accordingly, I wrote three letters: one to my friend to thank him; one to the Consul at Zurich applying for the job, but adding that "my shorthand was a bit rusty" and hoping that he would make allowances on that score. I asked for a month's grace, in order to give my Frankfurt employers notice. The third letter was to my mother in England to get for me and send post-haste all the Pitman shorthand books that the firm would recommend, after she had explained that I proposed to teach myself shorthand in four weeks.

The books arrived. The Consul engaged me. And Pitman never had a more assiduous devotee. Two hours before midnight and two after were the normal week-day ration of Pitman. By the time I arrived in Zurich my stenography was a hot-house hybrid affair of my own, grafted on to Pitman. But it served. It turned out that the principal part of my job was to do with the collection and compilation of statistics from Swiss Government departments and the writing of reports to the Board of Trade, for Milligan, the Consul, was also the British Government's "Commercial Agent" in Switzerland. In many ways I worked largely on my own and was Acting Vice-Consul when Milligan was away. We had an honorary Consul-General, Dr Angst, a distinguished Swiss ethnologist.

Zurich was the most German of the so-called German-Swiss towns, not because the Swiss had any particular affection for the Germans, but because the proportion of Germans to Swiss in it was very high. I found that the regional dialects differed very much from each other, and I have even known cases in which Swiss from one canton have had to talk to Swiss from another canton in High German in order to understand each other. School text-books were in High German, but out of school no boy or girl would dream of talking except in his native dialect.

I found a pension owned by a German widow. She and her two grannies spoke really good High German. The pension-naires were a mixed lot, but we all spoke German among ourselves. From my window I looked out on the domed Enge church with its lofty campanile. Enge was a quiet little suburb of Zurich which itself was a quiet though busy town, remarkably clean. But this was before the invasion of the motor car.

There was at one time quite a collection of Russians in the pension: some were students, some were anarchists, and all of them were dreamy reformers. Conversations on righting all that was wrong in the world would be continued on the bedroom stairs, after the sitting room was closed, well into the night. They did not stay very long and I think Frau Liebetanz, the proprietress, was not sorry to see them go. Germans and Austrians were birds of passage.

Of the more permanent residents the most noteworthy was Wladimir Ghidionescu. I have already referred to him as Roumanian Minister of Education when he met my sister at an international conference in 1932. As I knew him in 1905 he was black-bearded and enthusiastic. Ghi, as we called him, lived in the clouds—the nebulosities of Kant, Fichte, Hegel and company, from whose works he would recite chosen passages in German. Everybody liked him, for he was invariably polite. He was very absent-minded, and on one occasion, wishing to consult some professor at Jena, he got into an excursion train and found himself in Berlin.

Ghi's recreations were two: one was going to the Zurich theatre to hear Wagner's operas. I say "hear" because he used to lean back in his seat with closed eyes throughout the performance. This, he told me, was the best way to visualize and understand what Wagner meant, for the psycho-physical significance could never be reproduced on the stage. He instanced the voluptuously surging love-theme in *Tristan und Isolde*.

"But," I said, "Wagner wrote his works as music drama for performance by singers on a stage in a theatre."

This he admitted but said that in his opinion Wagner must have been fully conscious of the stage limitations for Valkyries riding through clouds and Rhine maidens swimming under water.

"Consequently," Ghi would argue, "when you have seen *The Ring*, for instance, once or twice, you don't need to fix your eyes on the performers or the setting. They are, in a way, disturbing elements. You should close your eyes and use your imagination."

Perhaps recreation is the wrong word for Ghi's other mood. Mild dissipation might best describe it. Once or twice a week he would appear at the dinner table with no appetite. We all knew what had happened and he would be duly chaffed: which he took in good part. What had happened was that at about 4 o'clock in the afternoon he had gone to Sprüngli's *Confiserie am Paradeplatz* and consumed large cups of chocolate and many pastries.

Ghidionescu had been a student at the Sorbonne before starting on his round of German and Swiss universities. Like all educated Roumanians, he spoke French fluently, so much so that he thought in French when he conversed in German. Thus, he never learnt to say "How do you do?" in the normal German fashion *Wie geht's Ihnen?* (more formal than *Wie geht's?*, for Ghi was punctiliously polite). He used to think *Comment allez-vous?* and translate literally *Wie gehen Sie?* which means "How are you walking?" To which Frau Liebetanz would reply, keeping a very straight face, that she was contriving to walk very well. Then she would burst out laughing and Ghi would smile deprecatingly.

He had married a French girl, a fellow student, while in Paris and the tragedy of his wife's death in childbirth left its mark on his temperament, which became one of deep melancholy, for he was passionately fond of her. His emotional affection was then concentrated on their son, who, when I knew Ghi in Zurich, was under the care of Ghi's parents in Bucharest. I once asked Ghi if he had any idea of the career he would like his son to follow.

"I want him to be an artist," he replied without a moment's hesitation.

"Why an artist?" I enquired.

"Because only an artist is really free," he replied with deep conviction.

I observed the same conviction whenever he spoke about Roumania. He never did this at table or in company with our fellow boarders. But when we were alone he would answer my questions.

"I imagine Roumania is the happiest of the countries in the Balkan peninsula," I said to him one day.

"We shall never be happy as a nation," he replied, "until our lost provinces are restored to us. Our thoughts are always 'over the mountains' in Transylvania—in the territories of which Hungary has robbed us."

"And what about Russia?" I asked.

"Yes," he said. "There are Moldavian territories too." But I could see that it was not this region that bothered him. His "heart was in the highlands"—of Transylvania.

For several years after we both left Zurich we used to correspond; but as neither of us stayed in the same place for very long, our correspondence came to an end. The peace treaties of 1919 gave back to Roumania the territories Ghi had pined for, thus doubling her population and the area of the kingdom. When I was in Dalmatia in 1914 Roumanian contingents passed through on their way to Albania to protect Prince Wied, the Prussian puppet ruler of that country. I had a chat with the officer in command. Ghidionescu had never mentioned to me that Roumania was particularly interested in Albania.

"Why should Roumania be sending troops to protect the new king of Albania?" I asked the officer.

"It isn't really quite like that," said the officer smiling. "The matter is more personal. Prince Wilhelm von Wied is the nephew of our Queen." I had forgotten that Carmen Sylva was Elizabeth von Wied.

In our Zurich pension there was a very pretty young Italian lady, from whom I began learning some Italian when we should both have been perfecting our German. A middle-aged Hungarian lady, who smoked a large cigar after dinner, was excellent company. She spoke several languages. Her husband, from whom she was apparently separated, used to visit her occasionally. Husband and wife were evidently good friends if they lived apart. He was Austrian, courteous as all educated Austrians are, and an entertaining raconteur. He was constantly travelling and had many stories to tell. I gathered he represented an armaments firm, for he had many contacts with army people in Germany. Our many defeats in the Boer War were much in my mind. Without referring to that war, I asked him what his opinion of the German Army was.

"As a military machine," he said, "I should say it is perfect: in organization and readiness far superior to our Army in Austria and to the French too. As to actual fighting, only a war could tell how much that superiority counts."

"They always seem so sure of their invincibility," I said.

"Yes, but one can never be sure," said the Austrian. "For instance, never was an army so badly organized or so ill prepared for fighting in South Africa as yours. Yet in the end you pulled it off. I don't know that the Germans would have done any better. Their whole preparation is for a European war, not for one in some other continent. That is what they talk about in their officers' messes in Berlin."

"Don't they ever let up from war talk?" I asked. "I thought there was plenty of Wine, Woman, and Song."

"Oh, there's plenty of wine; they can be very hospitable in their stiff way. But there's not much song."

"And plenty of woman?" I said laughingly.

"Yes, there's that too," said the Austrian. "But the really *chic* thing to do after a hectic dinner party in the officers' mess is to seek out not ladies, but lads, of easy virtue."

A Swiss lady, who had been governess in an Italian family for some years, spoke the most precise High German one could wish for. A young Italian marquis, who had been one of her charges as a child, used to come and visit her. They would chatter away in Italian, he always treating her with great deference.

Another permanent resident was a Swiss engineer. He was a passionate mountaineer and very muscular; but modest and courteous. We became great friends. One day we were talking in his room.

"How is it," I said to him, "that with all the business worries you tell me you have, you can go straight from your drawing board, every week-end, and climb mountains? That must put a great strain on your heart."

"Oh no," he said. "Look!" He got up from his chair, picked up a heavy dumb-bell, bent down, lifted it above his head, and lowered it slowly to the ground.

"My dear Ruegg," I said, "I don't think that proves anything except that you are very imprudent to do what you have just done so soon after lunch."

Ruegg spoke beautiful High German; in fact, as he told me once, better than he spoke his regional Zurich dialect. He had taken his engineering degree in Munich.

"I notice you haven't a single scar on your face," I said to him one day. "I suppose that, as a Swiss, you were exempt from the usual student duelling."

"On the contrary," he rejoined. "I probably did more duelling than the others."

"How comes it then that you have no scars?"

"As a matter of fact," said Ruegg, "I have a scar," and he parted his hair to show a scar. "I had drunk too much that day," he added.

"You must have been an expert swordsman," I said admiringly.

"Not really," he replied. "What happened was this. When I did my Swiss military service before going to Munich, I took lessons from the regimental fencing master. He taught me an infallible trick of disarming an opponent. The duels lasted 15 minutes; in some cases 20. But I could always disarm an opponent when I wanted."

Ruegg died of a heart attack one day. The funeral was delayed until a sister of his in England arrived. After the funeral she stayed some days at the pension before returning to England. She was a gay person, employed in the household of Ivan Caryll who at the time was musical director at the Gaiety and Lyric theatres in London and much in vogue as a composer of musical comedies like *The Shop Girl* and *The Circus Girl*.

Miss Ruegg apologized for not speaking English more fluently than she did.

"You see, we talk so much French in Mr Caryll's house," she said.

"Why?" I asked.

"Because Mr Caryll is really Belgian. He was born at Liège. His name is Félix Tilkin."

A young Dutch medical student whom I saw a lot of was Gerhardt van Ruysch. His father was Minister of the Interior and had sent him to spend a few months to escape from what Goethe called *das ewig Weibliche*, which had led him, as he told me, into many pranks and considerable scandal. In Zurich he was a reformed character! He studied assiduously; but failed to interest me in anything medical. He thought— this was in 1906—that sex changing might become quite common "in fifty years' time."

One day he came to my room and exclaimed: "I really cannot stand this country any more."

"What's wrong with it?" I asked.

"Oh, these awful hills and mountains. They overhang you. I feel as if I were in prison. I long to stand on one of our dunes and see for miles and miles and miles all round. And breathe."

"Pining for s'Gravenhage," I said, trying to pronounce the word in the guttural way he had been at pains to teach me.

"Yes," he replied quite seriously. "I must go back to my father."

"The Prodigal Son?" I said.

The last I heard of Ruysch he was a doctor in the Dutch Army and happily married.

One day in the Consulate Milligan handed me a private letter, the lines of which all sloped downwards. The writing was clear and the letter was signed Acton. This Lord Acton was the son of the historian. The latter had married the heiress of the Duke of Dalberg, whose wife was the daughter of a Genoese marquis.

Lord Acton, writer of the letter I have mentioned, was as English as King Edward VII, to whom and to King George V he was Lord-in-Waiting. He was born in Bavaria in 1870 and declared a British subject by Act of Parliament in 1911. The date is of some interest, because he had been appointed a Clerk in the Foreign Office twenty years earlier, and in 1911 was already our Chargé d'Affaires at the Hague. When he wrote the letter to Milligan he was Chargé d'Affaires at Berne. The letter itself was merely a humorous complaint of the damp cold at Berne and an enquiry whether there was any place near Zurich where the sun occasionally shone. We fixed him up at the Zürichberg which faces south-west, and he came to see us at the Consulate—a pleasant, bearded man with a ready smile.

Some years later, I met him again, this time at Berne when the first World War was raging. The reason Milligan asked me to peruse Acton's letter was that he wanted to air a theory of his. People who wrote with a downward slope, he maintained, betrayed pessimism, instability, and much else that I have forgotten. I attached no importance to this, merely remarking that it showed, in Acton's case, that he did not make use of the heavily lined underlay universally in use then to keep one in the straight. Milligan himself used it! It is not for me to judge, but I should say that in Lord Acton's case Milligan's theory was not made out at all.

A few days before Lord Acton had come to see us, Sir

William Conyngham Greene, our Minister at Berne, had called at the Consulate-General on his way to Bucharest, to which he had been transferred. In 1896 he had been seconded from the Foreign Office to the Colonial Office to be H.M. Agent at Pretoria, and he had left the Transvaal in October, 1899, "on the interruption of relations with the South African Republic." In my modest capacity I could not venture to have more than a few words with him, but having vivid recollections of the incidents of the Boer War I risked one question.

"Did you find the Boers very difficult to get on with, sir?"

"Yes, in many ways, though not personally," he replied. He had a very quiet, but very deliberate way with him, I noticed. "No argument would shake them," he went on. "Their political views and their religious beliefs were inextricably mixed up; so they were obstinate. However, that is all past history. But it will take some time for things to settle down in South Africa."

Chapter IV

*I*N MAY of 1906 the Simplon Tunnel was opened. To travel
through it was considered an adventure, and to celebrate
the opening there was an Exhibition at Milan. Having a
fortnight's holiday, I travelled from Zurich to Milan by the
St Gotthard railway and returned by the Simplon Tunnel. It
was June, and Milan was very, very hot. I did a lot of walking
and did not, at first, pay much attention to which side of the
street I walked on; but it was not long before I discovered why
the Italians say that dogs and Englishmen walk in the sun. I
learnt to choose the shady side. In this, to me, new world there
was much to admire: for instance the *Cimitero Monumentale*,
where what struck me most was a marble group representing
Christ driving out the moneylenders from the Temple. The
person buried beneath this immense monument could hardly
be a banker, I thought; perhaps a polemicist. The inscription
did not say. I remembered while walking round that an
Italian from Genoa, who used to visit our flat in London,
was never tired of talking of *"Genova Superba,"* and was emphatic
in affirming that the Milanese monumental cemetery was as
nothing compared with that at Genoa. I believe patriotic
parochialism is common to all nations.

My time in Milan was all too short. There was the Cathedral
to be visited and re-visited. There was the *Galleria Vittorio
Emmanuele* in which to sit and rest, and there were, of course,
thousands of Italians to be observed. I mention this because
when Ruskin was in Italy he does not seem to have come

across a single Italian; merely Italian architecture for which, apparently, he did not much care.

Coming out of the Cathedral one afternoon I saw a horse-drawn, open landau coming slowly across the *Piazza del Duomo*. Two ladies were in it and one of them was bowing gracefully to cheering people. Royalty to-day seems to have definitely adopted the uplifted arm with which to acknowledge plaudits. The lady acknowledging the cheers was Queen Margherita, who bowed as regally as Queen Alexandra used to. It was evident that the Italian queen-mother, then in her 55th year, was very popular, for this was no formal occasion. The queen, I imagine, was merely going shopping. From the attitude of the bystanders on that occasion and from what friends of mine at Domodossola told me, a few days later, I believe most Italians would have endorsed a French authority's pen portrait of Queen Margherita: *"Fort belle, d'une rare intelligence, très instruite, elle sut conquérir l'affection des Italiens par son charme, son affabilité, son inépuisable bienfaisance."* There is no doubt that for the Italian people this Princess of Savoy-Genoa and niece of the first king of a united Italy was a "real Italian." Her son's wife, Queen Helen, daughter of the Montenegrin chieftain Nicholas, was regarded as "foreign."

I could not hope to hear an opera in the Scala, for it was not the season; but there was to be a Sunday afternoon concert in aid of one of the many charities patronized by Queen Margherita. I climbed up to a place among the gods. The concert opened with a Beethoven symphony, and later on there was a piece by Elgar, for which, as a patriotic young Englishman, I felt pleased. In the middle of the Beethoven symphony I was astonished to see the conductor rap his desk. The orchestra stopped playing. Then it struck up the *Marcia Reale*. The conductor had half turned to a box on his left. Queen Margherita had just come in. When the music of the march had been played there was some discreet hand clapping. The queen bowed in acknowledgement and Beethoven's symphony was resumed. I remember thinking that the conductor had been guilty of *lèse*-Beethoven.

Some months later when I was in England I called on my

old choirmaster, Dr Charles Macpherson, and told him of my visit to the Scala. I showed him the programme.

"Did they like the Elgar piece?" he asked.

"They applauded," I said, "though perhaps not so warmly as they did some of the other items of the programme."

"Of course, they wouldn't understand Elgar. Over their heads" was Macpherson's comment. I think the disdain was misplaced.

On my way north after leaving Milan, I stopped at Domodossola to stay with some Italian friends. It was a very quiet little place. The head of the family with whom I stayed was a man of some substance, a *commendatore*, owner of Carrara marble quarries. Most of my short stay was in company with his son and daughter, whom I had known in Switzerland. On one occasion when the *commendatore* and I went for a stroll alone he impressed on me how lucky I was to be an Englishman, "the son of a country with liberal ideas—I mean politically progressive". On that topic I was rather out of my depth, certainly as regards Italy. So after saying how much I had enjoyed my short stay in Italy and what I had seen there, I said I gathered he thought Italy politically backward.

"But is there anything special which prevents Italy being, as you call it, politically progressive?" I asked.

"The Clericals," he replied, as though those two words explained everything. The year was 1906.

I wanted to sit below Mont Blanc and admire it: not climb it; so after my stay in Domodossola I interrupted my return to northern Switzerland by walking to Chamonix from Martigny over the Col de la Forclaz. It took me twelve hours. I came back next day in eight.

It was nearly two years since I had left England and my time in Zurich was getting short. I was going to regret leaving it, more especially because of the plentiful supply of good music. The municipal orchestra gave frequent concerts, and even if one did not pay to sit in the Tonhalle Gardens one could always sit on a bench by the lake and hear the music. This was the Zurich of no motor cars and of blue trams.

In the Municipal Theatre gallery places were cheap. Operas

64

were frequent, particularly Wagner. The local cast was good, the opera house being rated an *Uebergangsbuehne*—a sort of half-way house for singers who had performed at the smaller German opera houses and were hoping for engagements at Dresden, Leipzig, and so on.

In addition, there were engagements of guest-singers like Maria Gay, for instance, who sang *Carmen*. I went to hear her with one of my Hungarian friends—the musical one. He was quite as enthusiastic as I was about her singing, but did not fail to point out, as he munched an outsize German ham sandwich during the interval, that it was a pity she was "so large round here," and he described a wide circle round his hips with the sandwich. Maria Gay sang in French, while the local singers sang in German. The effect was sometimes curious. In the first Act when Carmen sets out to inveigle José, he is sitting astride a chair pretending not to notice her and twisting some flowers into a chain.

"*Qu'est-ce que tu fais?*" she asks him. His reply: "*Ich mache eine Kette*" came as a shock.

I once assisted at a performance at Zurich in which three languages were used. It was when Henri Albers of the Théâtre de la Monnaie in Brussels came to Zurich to sing *Rigoletto*. He sang in Italian. Another guest artist, whose name I do not recall, sang in French. The local cast sang in German. But when, after the Duke has carried off Rigoletto's daughter, the courtiers mock the jester with the words "*Was gibt's neues, du Narr?*" Henri Albers, instead of snarlingly throwing back their gibe at them in Italian, did so in German. The effect was doubly dramatic. After that, he continued in Italian, and the opera proceeded in three languages. Incidentally, the only Gilda I ever saw who really looked the part, was the silver-toned Barrientos. This was in Rio de Janeiro, and so delicately fragile was she that the tenor did actually carry her off in the abduction scene, and did not have to use the dummy needed because of the embonpoint of most operatic Gildas.

On one occasion at Zurich we had the visit of the Keim Orchestra from Munich. The advance publicity they had was, I think, justified. They occupied the stage at the Municipal

65

Theatre, and one of the pieces they played was the *Liebestod* music from *Tristan und Isolde*. The applause was loud and long. The conductor bowed and bowed again; so did the orchestra. But the audience insisted on an encore. The conductor lifted his bâton and the music began all over again. After the first two bars of it, he left the podium and sat immobile on a chair facing the audience. The orchestra played the whole thing just as well as they had done the first time. Ever since that experience I have sometimes wondered whether the antics of some conductors are really necessary on the night of the concert.

In December I said goodbye to Switzerland and went home. I took with me the piano score of a new Viennese operetta, which I and my Hungarian friend had been to see twice when it came to Zurich. It was called *Die Lustige Witwe*. What will it be called when it comes to London? we wondered. "The Gay Widow," I said. I was wrong. The German translation of *The Merry Wives of Windsor* should have given me the clue.

* * *

After spending the Christmas holidays with my mother and sister in London I crossed over to Paris. My difficulty in this case was that I had no commercial introductions, and as the idea was that my career should be banking, though the idea never smiled on me, it was business experience and not academic connexions which I had to seek in Paris. Yet the only recommendation I took with me to Paris was an academic one: it was to the widow of a Sorbonne professor. The result was that during my first three weeks in Paris I found myself living in a pension in the Boulevard St Germain. It was in a solid Second Empire construction, and the rooms were high and large. I occupied a small attic. I was not unduly impressed with the knowledge that I was living in a quarter of Paris famous for its literary and historical associations. What concerned me was how to find a job.

Meanwhile, I was making friends with some of my fellow guests at the pension. One was an Italian journalist from

Sinalunga, which he was most anxious that one should not confuse with Siena. Sinalunga, he insisted, was of equal historical interest, though so very much smaller. Italian patriotism is still to this day largely a matter of civic pride: and none the worse for that. I asked him his opinion of Antonio Fogazzaro, two of whose novels I had read. His opinion was that Fogazzaro was certainly an entertaining writer, but that he would never become a classic. In any case, he said, he was much more read outside Italy than by Italians.

The pension was quite a small one, in effect a family affair in which we were paying guests. There was the lady of the house, whose two daughters were away at school all day; the Italian journalist; a young French student; and myself. The other guests, Chapman by name, were an American family, distinguished by that spontaneous cordiality so characteristic of educated people from the United States. They were obviously people in easy circumstances. Mrs Chapman, a widow, had a grown-up son and daughter with her. The son, who had studied to be an architect, was in Europe to look round and become familiar with French architecture. He was a young man of about 23 and was accompanied by a college friend, Trautschold, who did not appear to be studying anything in particular. Trautschold was a very slow-speaking man, with a slight stutter. He came to visit us one evening a year later at my mother's flat in Hampstead. On that evening, as it happened, an old friend of ours from Yorkshire, Bradshaw, a middle-aged bachelor, was visiting us too. He was a man of means and his amusement was travelling. He knew Paris well. This is how some of the conversation went that evening:

Bradshaw (quickly): How did you like your time in Paris?

Trautschold (deliberately): Very much. I don't speak any French, but people were always very pa— pa——

Bradshaw (impatient): Helpful.

Trautschold (taking his time): —patient.

Bradshaw: I don't talk any foreign language either. Yet I am constantly travelling in foreign countries.

Trautschold: Don't you find the lack of a foreign language an im— im——

Bradshaw (impatient): A hindrance? No.

Trautschold (taking his time): —impediment. I did manage to pick up a few French, a few— a few——

Bradshaw (impatient): Words.

Trautschold (with great deliberation): A few phrases. But my pronunciation is very in— very in——

Bradshaw (impatient): Poor.

Trautschold: Very inferior.

My mother and I had to intervene from time to time during the rest of the evening not merely to keep the talk moving, but to resist the temptation to laugh outright.

But to return to Paris. The widowed American lady had a brother with her, apparently a bachelor, in any case unattached. He used to frequent the American Embassy, to which his sister went but rarely. She seemed to be a bit of an invalid. When the bachelor brother had been to an Embassy reception alone, he would describe in detail, next day, to his sister and niece the costumes worn by the women the night before. He may have been a professional costumier; but I think his delight in describing the dresses was too glowing for that.

I paid my first visit to the Louvre with them. Standing before the Mona Lisa, the uncle held forth at great length on its wonders. It sounded to me like guide-book stuff.

"Isn't this a bit boring?" I whispered to the young lady.

"Yes," she whispered back; "but Uncle Ned is always very insistent that we must see and admire all the things we are supposed to see and admire in Paris."

Uncle Ned confided to me one day that the house in which we were living on the Boulevard St Germain was the one in which Marat had been murdered. The house and its neighbours dated only from the Haussmann era; but I had soon got to know that Uncle was full of *idées fixes* and that it was much more pleasant not to argue. He had some wild ideas about Ariadne too, much wilder even than some of the conflicting legends about the

lady. These he aired before taking a box at the Opera for a
performance of Massenet's *Ariane*, at which he was kind enough
to ask me to join them. Having been soaked in Wagner at
Zurich I confess I found Massenet rather flat. But I learned to
appreciate the French composer better later on.

I think the Chapmans thought my French wonderful, for
they had none. But though I was glad to be of some service to
these delightful people, I was not making any progress in
getting a job. It was not for lack of trying. I read *Le Journal*
every day. It carried a clever short story which I enjoyed
reading. Occasionally I read *Le Matin* too. Its offices occupied
the whole of a big building, all red paint and glass, on the
Grands Boulevards, and it was currently said that it was far
easier to be received by the President of the Republic than by
the editor of *Le Matin*. In which he was, no doubt, wiser than
the editor of *Le Figaro*, M. Calmette, who was shot dead in his
office by Mme Caillaux in March, 1914.

Political campaigns were carried on with great virulence in
the Paris press, and politicians and other public men in France
did not, as in England, hide behind the law of libel or seek
pecuniary profit by invoking it. They gave in one paper as
good as they got in another. When I was in Paris, for instance,
Georges Clemenceau was Minister of the Interior. Apart from
an anti-clerical campaign, there had been strikes and much
violence, and the Military had been called out to restore order.
To judge by the articles in some of the newspapers one would
have gathered that Clemenceau had literally been wading in
blood. One illustrated paper did actually portray Clemenceau
doing just that. But it never occurred to Clemenceau to bring
a libel action against the author of the lampoon.

I went through the usual moods of depression when my
searches for work were unsuccessful. But one day my luck
turned. A young French business man I called on in answer to
an advertisement for a "business associate"—the kind of
position I had no right to apply for!—recommended me to a
friend of his. My troubles were over. Edmond Tournier, a man
of about 35, was the Paris representative of a number of French
provincial firms dealing in *articles de Paris*. He was also buying

agent in Paris for a firm in Hanover Square, London, trading under the name of Fleury Frères. The brothers' real name was Levin, and they bought not only for the British market, but for the Canadian market too. The work in Tournier's business consisted of calling on many wholesale firms in Paris every day. Tournier had been ordered by his doctors to spend some months continuously in the South of France. Even so, he was a bundle of energy. He had one assistant, Jean Mercier, a young Frenchman a year or two older than myself. We two would carry on Tournier's business while he was away: I to look after the London end, since Jean knew no English. Jean and I became the very best of friends. I soon picked up the hang of the business from him, and, later on when he was away ill for several weeks, managed to carry on quite alone, except for the office boy, a lively and helpful youngster.

Tournier's office was on the ground floor of a building in the rue du Faubourg Poissonnière, the third house from the big boulevards. It was to a pension almost opposite that I transferred myself from the Boulevard St Germain, and once again, I had an attic. It was cheaper! The pension was run by an elderly French couple with the help of a girl from the provinces. The food was first-rate and ample. That being so, I was not really surprised when I found that my fellow-pensionnaires were mostly German. We talked a lot of German as well as French, and as they were all in various businesses, banks, insurance companies, and commission houses, I picked up quite a lot of useful information about business in Paris.

My friends, however, were French: Jean and his friends. And splendid fellows they were! One of the best of the fellows was Jeanne, who was Jean's girl friend. She was a cutter in a ready-made clothing factory. Jean was a mass of nerves, thin, excitable. Jeanne was calm and unruffled, full of common sense, and a loyal companion. She was a pretty brunette, and Jean's mother, a widow, was very fond of her, for she kept Jean straight and from falling too easily to the wiles of other women. Another companion was Jules, a fair-headed muscular Norman, who was doing his three years' military service as a fireman in Paris. And there was Maurice, in many ways the most interesting, because the most unexpected, character of our Bohemian circle. There was nothing of Henri Murger's *Vie de Bohème* in our life. We were all workers, all relatively poor—centimes counted!—all good friends, and our gatherings were frank and free.

We used to meet at about 6 o'clock on Sunday morning, during the fine weather, and cycle to Fontainebleau, Versailles, or elsewhere, so that I got to know the surrounding districts of Paris very well. Sometimes we would go further afield, to Gisors, for instance, and cycle back all night. The general idea was to have Sunday in the country. One of the party was cashier and bought the picnic lunch and the drinks. Then on Monday evening we would meet and settle our accounts. Sometimes on hot summer nights we would buy Chinese lanterns, hang them on our handle bars, and pedal through the Bois de Boulogne to Suresnes, where one could dance to music from phonographs or, more often, from piano and fiddle.

Jean and Jeanne rode a tandem. Maurice was the expert cyclist of the party. He stripped mud-guards off my Rudge-Whitworth, removed all other superfluous weight, and lowered the handle-bars. I learnt a lot about bicycling from him. Indeed I learnt a lot about a lot of things from this little group of friends. I learnt the meaning of true companionship. They admitted me to be one of themselves in the most natural and unostentatious manner possible. Above all things, they were frank and unaffected.

Maurice was quite a character: a fanatic cyclist in his spare time; he could have been a bicycle acrobat I believe. He was tall and wiry, dark-haired, with darting brown eyes in an unprepossessing face. His views were sensible and down to earth and his language uncompromising. Jean was blue-eyed, fresh complexioned, with blonde wavy hair. He would have been handsome, had he not had a Habsburg chin; but he was handsome enough to attract the ladies. Maurice was a highly-skilled artisan in a machine-tools works. He lived with his family in a modest apartment on the Left bank. The first World War made victims of these companions, whose memory I cherish.

Tournier, my chief, dark-haired, impulsive, and always friendly, I used to visit at Asnières where he had a small property. It was during one of his many absences at Nice and while Jean was away on holiday that I decided to leave the pension opposite the office. I had grown rather tired of the German crowd there, who could talk of nothing but their business affairs and would persist in bullying the maid-of-all-work. With Maurice's help I found rooms in the Vaugirard district. The distance between my new quarters and the pension was considerable—a matter of four miles. I could cycle across Paris, in fact I did so frequently; but removal of books and luggage would entail some expense.

"Don't bother," said Maurice. "I'll borrow a barrow. We'll put your things on it, bike and all, and trundle it across Paris on Sunday. And we can stop at a couple of bistros on the way." That was typical of Maurice, always ready to help and always practical. I had visions of being stopped by an *agent de police*: two suspicious characters, reasonably well dressed, pushing a barrow, loaded with stolen goods perhaps. However, we had no *stoppage in transitu*, except at the two bistros. I believe the rue Vaugirard is the longest street in Paris. I was quite sure it was by the time we reached our destination.

One day at the office, Andrews, the buyer for Canada, turned up, sent to Paris by the Hanover Square firm of Fleury Frères. He asked me to dinner, and Tournier told me I had better take him to the Folies Bergère afterwards. "That is where he usually wants to go," he said.

"Oughtn't *you* to be taking him there?" I said.

"*Jamais de la vie*," replied Tournier. "Those places are only for the foreign visitor. It is what the foreign visitor expects to find; so it is provided for him. You won't see a Frenchman in the place." Which, of course, is not strictly true. But it is true that French business men did not frequent such shows. They lived a quiet bourgeois life at Suresnes or Asnières. I duly went with the buyer from Canada. It was a dull evening. He was mum and glum. Most depressing.

I had another depressing evening when a buyer, Craddock, from one of the big London department stores came to Paris with a business friend. He had no interest in Tournier's line of business. He looked me up because he was a friend of ours in London. He was a bachelor, very English. Paris had no attractions for him. He stayed only twenty-four hours to do his business. He asked me to "choose a good place for us to dine." Tournier had once taken me to Marguéry's, near the Porte St Martin, where *sole Marguéry* was the famous speciality. Monsieur Marguéry, then an old man, walked round the tables and hoped everything, meaning his famous sole, was to one's liking. It was a meal in itself. But my friend and his companion wanted steaks and beer, and when we returned to their hôtel in the rue de Rivoli drank whisky and talked about a whist drive at their boarding house in Streatham.

On two occasions I sat in the gallery of the Porte Saint-Martin theatre to enjoy Rostand's *Cyrano de Bergerac* with Coquelin *aîné* in the title-rôle. A year later, I saw the company give the same play at His Majesty's Theatre, London. M. Jacques Charon, director of the Comédie-Française, stated recently that it was more realistic that Cyrano should be played by a younger actor than Coquelin, who was in his 50's when he created the part. Perhaps the author of the play can have the last word. The play was first produced at the Porte Saint-Martin theatre on December 28, 1897, and on the fly-leaf of the 1908 printed edition are these words:

C'est à l'âme de CYRANO que je voulais dédier ce poème. Mais puisqu'elle a passé en vous, COQUELIN, c'est à vous que je le dédie. E.R.

I learnt much of Rostand's play by heart and used to amuse my companions by apostrophizing them as

. . . les cadets de Gascogne,
Bretteurs et menteurs sans vergogne.

My sister, who was already lecturing in mathematics, had to do some teaching in French too; so she and my mother decided to spend a short holiday in France. A Girton friend of my sister's who was studying at Rennes introduced her to the widow of a Sorbonne professor. In the summer months this lady received pensionnaires at an old farm house she owned at

St Valéry-sur-Somme. I cycled there to spend a week-end
with them. Madame Sauvageot's farm house, with its red-
tiled floors and oak beams, was an attractive place. She was a
white-haired lady of about sixty, highly cultivated and mildly
despotic. Guests came recommended to her from all over the
world. From October to March she lived in Paris. A daughter
looked after the household chores at St Valéry, aided by a cook
and a maid.

There was Marc, too, a French youth of about seventeen
on whom Mme Sauvageot doted. He may have been the son of
her daughter. It was a point that was never established. And
there was Tunis. Marc and Tunis were inseparable. Tunis
was a small donkey, a most attractive animal presumably
named after the land of his birth. Marc was a student; but as
it was holiday-time he merely lounged about and occasionally
wrote poetry. Wherever he went Tunis was at his heels. We all
went to Mass on the Sunday I was there. In the middle of it I
heard a peculiar Clonk Clonk sound. I looked round. It was
Tunis who had come through the open door of the church in
search of Marc.

At the time of my visit the guests were two American ladies,
mother and daughter; a Japanese student; a mysterious man
from the Near East, whose nationality seemed undetermined—
some said he was a Syrian, others that he was a Turk (he
could have been both in those days); others said he came from
Egypt, others suggested Armenian. They asked me what I
thought. I suggested Amalekite. There were several young
English ladies, who used to gaze with rapture on the Amalekite
when, with Mme Sauvageot's permission, he made Turkish
coffee for them. Another guest was an Englishman holding a
high post in the Egyptian administration. He spoke French
quite passably, but told me he came to get sea air and
good French combined, for Mme Sauvageot spoke really
well.

Mme Sauvageot was clever in running her little pension
largely on self-service lines. On my first day there, lunch
being over, I noticed that there was a regular drill to a suitable
accompaniment of words. It went on these lines:—Mme

74

Sauvageot *loquitur*, in French: "We will push back our chairs, thus. Miss April will brush the crumbs from the table. Miss May will take the broom and sweep the floor. Mrs Jones will help clear away the things. Miss Hambloch will collect the plates. Miss Jones will collect the knives and forks. We must wash the dishes . . ." and so on, everybody suiting the action to the word of command. And certainly the job was done, and done cheerfully with much joking, in next to no time. Then the guests were left to their own devices, though to some Mme Sauvageot gave French lessons.

In the evening after dinner she would preside over a kind of *cercle*, the guests sitting round and suggestions being made as to who should do what to entertain the others. There was no piano, Mme Sauvageot's dictum being that a piano spoilt good singing. But, when I was there, nobody would sing without a piano. Did anybody dance? she asked. I wondered how people were to dance without music. But the younger American lady said she would oblige. What would she dance? The Dance of the Seven Veils. I was curious to see what would happen. The girl disappeared and came back with a long piece of green muslin. Then she cavorted about waving it and humming—all this in deadly earnest. Nothing lascivious about this plump maiden. But the Amalekite's eyes gleamed, and there was polite applause. Marc read a poem, and one of the English girls recited something. Then the group broke up. My mother and sister and I went for a stroll to enjoy the long summer evening.

It was all very amusing for a day or two, and I was glad to have been at the place from which William of Normandy set out for England. But I was glad to get back to Paris. This was the Paris of fiacres and giant omnibuses and of many curses at the smelly horseless, dust-raising motor contraptions that were beginning to appear on the streets—a growing danger to the unwary cyclist. It was the Paris of much tunnelling for the future *métro* extensions, of larger-than-life caricatures and gramophone music at shop entrances to attract customers and collect groups of *badauds*. It was the Paris of long hours of intensive work, and of study too; but the city of many pleasures:

the Paris of much simple gaiety—a city that fascinates and enslaves.

My departure was fixed for December. Jean told me that *toute la bande* had insisted on coming to the Gare St Lazare to see me off. We had a gay good-bye dinner. We all said it would not be good-bye. But it was.

Chapter V

The City Treadmill — Changing Horses — Cramming and Teaching
— From Windermere to Belgrade — Balkan turmoil.

I WAS in London. My old headmaster G. L. Bennett, true
to his promise, had reported me to his banker friend
Lehnmann as an Englishman with languages and education
for whom, so he told Bennett, he had hitherto looked in vain.
An interview with the great man in his bank in the City
followed, during part of which we spoke in German, his native
tongue. I felt much encouraged. He held out promises of a
rosy future. I could begin work on the following Monday. He
bent forward to deal with some papers on his desk. Evidently
I was expected to leave. I ventured to remind him that he
had not said anything about salary.

He sat back in his chair and looked up at me with as benevolent a mien as, I suppose, a banker can manage.

"You know," he said, "it will be a great privilege for you to
work in my bank."

"I am sure of that," I said.

"Now all these young men you saw as you passed through
just now," said the banker, "are only too pleased to come to me
and start as *volontaires*."

"I'm afraid I could not possibly do that," I told him. "I've
been earning enough to pay my way in Frankfurt, Zurich, and
Paris during the past three years. So, I must look for something
in England where I can do the same."

"Yes, yes," he said impatiently, "but a bank—my bank—is
something quite different from what you have been doing."
I said nothing. "Well, as an exception, quite as an exception,
you understand, I will pay you £7 a month."

I hesitated for a moment or two and then found myself

saying: "Very well, sir, and I am obliged to you for the opportunity."

The change from the life I had been used to—an active outdoor life—was abrupt. I felt like a prisoner at a treadmill. With the exception of two Belgians, all the junior clerks were German. So were the managers, of whom there were five. But the Foreign Exchange department was run by three Englishmen. When the "establishment" manager (he was Swiss) brought me round my pay packet with its exiguous contents, I saw that all the clerks had pay packets too. Obviously what Lehnmann had told me about *volontaires* was a fable. But after the first month I was put in the Foreign Exchange department, and that was to his credit. I liked working with the three men who ran it and I did learn a lot. I had charge of the Canadian desk, too, for a short spell. But after eight months of it I was quite sure I was not cut out for a bank life. I went in to see the great man and told him so. I could not resist reproaching him about the salary matter. On that he made no comment.

"So you are leaving," he said. "Well, what do you propose to do?"

"I don't know," I replied. "I have an idea that I might sit for some examination and get a job in Government service."

"The Government are bad payers," he said drily.

"No worse, I imagine, than you," I retorted. I could not resist the riposte. He bridled, and began talking German. There was no point in our discussing that. I might have gone far in his bank. I said I doubted it.

"In any case," he said, "I will give you a word of advice. In future don't change horses in mid-stream."

"That," I replied, "will depend on what sort of horse I am riding."

On looking through the summary of subjects set by the Civil Service Commissioners for the Consular Service exams, I realized that I could not hope to be successful, however hard I studied, without some coaching in mercantile law, commercial geography, and political economy. At the same time I had to

78

earn my living. I put my name down in a scholastic agency and then went to see a firm of crammers. Gibson, the head of it, was a large untidy man in an untidy office. His scholastic attainments were considerable and his knowledge of the wiles of examiners profound. He told me what books to buy and we at once began a correspondence course.

As I had no university degree the schools agency people were dubious of my ever getting a school job, but thought they could get me some coaching work in French and German. However, I was lucky. A day or two later they called me to interview a north country headmaster who had a sudden vacancy. Platt, the headmaster of Windermere Grammar School, told me he was not so keen on the degree business. "The man whose place you would take had good degrees, but he couldn't teach," said Platt. "I want someone who will get the boys through their exams." He got me, and the boys did get through their exams.

I liked the life at Windermere as a resident master, responsible for games as well as Latin, Greek, French, German, and Geography. In free time we climbed, rowed and cycled, besides playing cricket and football; and one winter we skated on Rydal Water.

"We are reminded that we are a grant-earning institution," said Platt one morning at breakfast. He had been reading the contents of a very official looking envelope.

"What does that imply?" I asked.

"It means that we get a subsidy or grant from the Board of Education, provided our teaching is up to the Board's standard of requirements. What it means for us at this moment is that an inspector from the Board—H.M.I. as we call them in the profession—will be descending on us next week."

When the H.M.I. did turn up, he sat at the back of the class during some of my lessons. I found he had taken a degree at Leipzig. He advised me to get a university degree by correspondence if I thought of making a career of teaching. "Parents like to see letters after a teacher's name on the school prospectus," he said smiling. I resolved in my own mind to follow his advice if I failed in the Consular exam.

Peter Paul Platt was a bachelor, moody and explosive; but a good sport.

"Who were the two ladies I saw you taking round the school yesterday?" I asked him one day. "Were they Board of Education people too?"

"No," said Platt. "They represented some welfare society busy comparing grammar schools and other schools." Then, after a characteristic chuckle, he went on. "They asked all kinds of questions and diligently chronicled my answers on some sort of questionnaire they had brought with them. But," and here he chuckled again, "one of their questions I found rather embarrassing."

"Let's have it," cried my colleagues at top table.

"Well, they asked me about discipline. I explained that we never gave Lines and really hardly ever had any trouble.

" 'But,' one of the old dears asked me, looking up from her questionnaire, 'do you never cane a boy?'

" 'Very, very rarely,' I told her.

" 'And when that happens, where do you cane the boy?' she asked.

" 'Here, in my study,' I told her.

" 'Ah yes,' she said sweetly. 'But I mean where—on the boy?'

That rather flummoxed me, so I blurted out, "Oh, I just make him bend over."

After I had been a year at Windermere Platt gave me leave to go to London to sit for the Consular exam. I went armed with books for last-minute cramming. My mother would have none of it.

"You are taking us to the theatre tonight," she said.

"But I have to sit for the first paper tomorrow," I protested. "I cannot possibly go to the theatre."

But I did. We went to the Gaiety and saw *Our Miss Gibbs*, the music of which ran pleasantly through my head during the following days while I wrestled with questions which I felt might have puzzled even Adam Smith, Ricardo, Chisholm, and all the law lords of England.

In September (1909) the results came out. Windermere

became a thing of the past, and in November, after a few weeks at the Foreign Office, I found myself in the British Legation at Belgrade.

Nothing could have been more auspicious for me than the fact that my first chief was Sir Beethom Whitehead. He and Lady Whitehead were the personification of kindness and hospitality to me, as indeed they were to everybody. They were deservedly the most popular diplomatists in Belgrade. (The wife of an envoy can be the most helpful of diplomatists.)

The year was 1909. By brutally annexing the Slav provinces of Bosnia and Herzegovina, which happened shortly before my arrival in Belgrade, the Austrians had broken every rule of the international game as then played. Feeling ran particularly high in Serbia against what the Serbs considered a deliberate provocation. Everything was on the boil in the Balkans, but it was precisely the Serb element which would cause the cauldron to boil over into European and world war, though it was the Dual Monarchy which had kindled the flames.

While I was in Belgrade there were frequent demonstrations, there was partial mobilization, and there was war talk. At the Legation we were kept busy with despatches and cypher telegrams. The Legation staff consisted of three people: the Minister, myself, and an Austrian porter. A young bi-lingual lady—her father was Serb and her mother English—did translations for Sir Beethom. Forty years later, when the late Sir Charles Peake was home on leave from his post as Ambassador at Belgrade, I asked him, out of curiosity, how many people he had on his staff there. He thought a moment and then said: "Seventy," adding after another pause, "and I don't know what half of them do."

F

Chapter VI

Rio de Janeiro and Villegagnon — The last Imperial ball — The Emperor and the Army — The Army and the Republic — Oswaldo Cruz rids Brazil of Yellow Fever and introduces Hydrangeas to Petropolis — Haggard and his ways — Roger Casement, the Irish Consul — An English bullfighter — His quiver full of them — Congo and Putumayo stories — The Germans and Roger Casement.

M Y INSTRUCTIONS were to proceed to Rio de Janeiro with all speed. I was to take over the Consulate-General there from Roger Casement, who was pining to go on leave. Within a month of my arrival Casement left Rio for South Africa. He never returned, and I was left in charge of the Consulate-General for four years.

I found Rio de Janeiro very expensive. The local currency was the milréis, corresponding to the modern cruzeiro. It was worth 15 pence. In other words £1 was worth only 16 milréis. That was in 1910. In 1968 the £1 is worth over 6,000 cruzeiros (milréis). Such are the vagaries of foreign exchange. Exchange may be no robbery, but foreign exchange is often a great swindle.

My first acquaintance with trading stamps, merely a nodding one, was in Rio de Janeiro. I had come down from my hotel in Santa Thereza and was waiting for a tram to take me to dine with friends in Laranjeiras when I was surprised to see a large shop display brilliantly illuminated. There was no window. Shop windows came to Rio a little later. The show was full of household goods, cosmetics and tea sets, as well as much gimcrackery. But there was no movement in the shop: no salesmen and no customers. In large letters over the goods was one word BRINDES. It means a toast proposed at dinner, and it means, too, a gift or offering. Why, I asked myself, should

82

the firm whose name appeared under the word give things away? At dinner the lady of the house explained that these articles were "given" to the housewife who had bought other goods for which she had received stamps. Did this trade stamp device exist in Great Britain in 1910?

In that year the population of Brazil was 17 million. It had been 14 million in 1889, when the Republic was declared. By 1940 it had risen to 45 million, and by 1965 to over 80 million. Brazil's Statistical Institute estimates that by 1970 the population will have reached 95 million.

When I was travelling in Brazil during the First World War one of the passengers on my boat was the wife of a Brazilian business man whom I knew in Rio. They were both from Ceará. She told me she was very sad at having to leave her family even for a few days.

"Have you a large family?" I asked her.

"Oh no," she replied; "only eight children."

In one of my early letters home I mentioned quite casually that there were plenty of washer-women to be had, but that there was no laundry in the city. On receiving my letter, my mother apparently had serious thoughts of interesting a City friend of ours, Harlow, in forming a company to operate the first laundry in Brazil. But nothing came of the idea.

It was, however, not laundries which I talked of in my first letters home. It was the incomparable beauty of Rio de Janeiro, its surroundings, and its bay. This beauty has been rapidly modified in recent years by urbanists, planners, and (perhaps not even lastly, for worse may be coming) by building speculators. Sky-scrapers have been pushed down almost to the water's edge in Copacabana, for instance, leaving only a beggarly strip of promenade. This is periodically washed away by the Atlantic and has to be periodically repaired. The promenade is literally built on sand, and I once suggested to Dr Paulo Frontin, a distinguished Brazilian engineer and former Prefect of the City and district, that until the skyscrapers were one day washed away by a real tidal wave, it might be a good plan to build wooden groins, such as we have in English seaside beaches, to break the force of the Atlantic waves. There would be the additional advantage that they would provide some shade, of which there is none on the Copacabana beach. But Frontin said No; groins would spoil the beauty of the beach.

Even the most persistent efforts of futurist plotters and *avant-garde* designers will never, I imagine, succeed in completely spoiling the dramatically natural splendour of the immense bay of Guanabara, with the Sugar Loaf standing sentinel at its narrow entrance. The mountains sweep round in a grandiose curve from the west and there is the magnificent drop curtain of even higher mountains in the far distance to the north. The bay covers 150 square miles and is studded with 50 islands. The whole scene is gigantic and breath-taking.

When I arrived, in January, 1910, there were no aeroplanes and no docks. These were being built by a British firm. Slowly our steamer passed the island of Villegagnon, before dropping anchor near the Fiscal Island. Both these islands deserve a passing word.

Villegagnon is no longer an island. It has been joined to the mainland to become an air-port, named after Santos Dumont, the Brazilian aviator who preceded the Wright brothers as the first airman successfully to fly a heavier-than-air machine. No doubt, it is more useful to have an airport than an historical landmark. The island was named after the French Protestant adventurer who, had he been backed from Paris, might have succeeded in making a reality of the project of founding *La France Antarctique* from his headquarters on the island which he called Fort Coligny, after his friend and chief in Paris. It is characteristic of Brazilian tolerance that, having defeated Villegagnon and his project, they should have named the island after him.

The *Ilha Fiscal* is historical in another, and more modern, context. Its appearance is incongruous, or would be so if exotic scenery was not capable of absorbing into itself any and every eccentricity. It is as though the German, Norman, French, and Italian architects who worked on Milan Cathedral for nearly five hundred years, until Napoleon finished the job in 1813, had formed themselves into an unlimited liability company and decided to erect a combination of church, chapel, and monastery in Gothic style on a small island in the tropics.

The building occupies virtually the whole of the very small island. Under the Brazilian monarchy somebody had the brilliant idea that one of the best ways of preventing smuggling would be to house Customs officers on an island in the Bay of Rio itself. Small suspicious craft moving to and from Rio could easily be spotted from an island to which the appropriate name of Fiscal Island was given. Why the building for lodging the Customs officers should have been in the shape of a miniature Gothic cathedral was a point that nobody could explain to me. What was abundantly clear was that the scheme was unworkable. The planners, as is their wont, forgot something essential. They forgot that the Customs officials might prefer the company of their wives to the monastic dormitories of the island. The scheme was abandoned, but the island's title remained.

The *Ilha Fiscal* was part of the imperial patrimony, and, being close to the mainland, could be used for functions. When lit up at night for official *festas* the scene was fairy-like. Its historical interest is that it was the scene of the last ball given by the Emperor, only two days before the fall of the monarchy. When I arrived in Rio, Sir William Haggard was our Minister. Lady Haggard was the daughter of a former head of a British public utility enterprise in Rio de Janeiro. Haggard had met her years before when he was Secretary of Legation at Rio. Lady Haggard used to tell me what a gay occasion this last ball of the Brazilian Emperor had been. Dom Pedro II was invariably gracious to the British community and many of its leading members were in the Court visitors' book. It was a hot summer night in November, 1889, when Miss Hancox went with her parents to the ball on the Fiscal Island. What struck the future Lady Haggard particularly on looking back, she told me, was that there had not been the slightest inkling, not a murmur, not a hint of the impending change of régime.

In historical retrospect that is understandable. Like so many historical events, the declaration of the Republic was an accident. Even on the day itself, November 15, 1889, the man who proclaimed the Republic had not the slightest intention of doing so when he got out of bed in the morning. The Brazilian painter Henrique Bernardelli has depicted Marshal Deodoro da Fonseca in an heroic posture on horseback, but the sober truth is that this officer was not a republican at all. He was a general with a grievance—was there ever a general in any country without one?—and with a grudge against the Imperial cabinet. I have dealt elsewhere* at some length with the change from a monarchy to a republic in Brazil. But an outline of the events leading up to it will not be out of place here, because when I arrived in Brazil in 1910 all the older members of the British community had lived under the Monarchy, and I met many Brazilians who were monarchists at heart or at least doubtful of the wisdom of the change to republicanism.

The most ardent of the republican propagandists in the 1880's was a man known as Benjamin Constant. Like all officers, he had sworn allegiance to the Emperor at the outset of his military career. That is an aspect which need not concern us here; but I will take the opportunity to clear up a confusion that exists about Christian and other names in the minds of many people who to-day write about Brazil and their impressions of its people. "The Brazilian dictator-president Getúlio Dornelles Vargas (1930-45 and 1951-54) is known by his Christian name, which is proof of his popularity." Statements like this are repeated by many foreign writers on Brazil. Whether Getúlio Vargas was popular or not is beside the point. Some people he favoured, some he exiled, and some he clapped into jail or handed over to his Chief of Police to be dealt with in the tortuous ways typical of any dictator's police force. He was, of course, a past master in the art of demagogy. He created two Labour parties, so that the masses hugged the illusion that he was their particular friend, on the lines of "the good angel, Spenlow, whose heart and hand would have always been open, but for the restraining demon, Jorkins."

*In *His Majesty the President*.

Brazil has had about sixteen presidents since she became a republic and half of them have been referred to in Brazil by their first name, not for reasons of affection, but simply because that is the custom of the country. For instance, the president whom Getúlio Vargas deposed in 1930 was known as Washington Luiz, and few people in Brazil then or now could tell you his full name: Washington Luiz Pereira de Souza. A war-time president was (1914–18) Wenceslão Braz Pereira Gomes, but to all his compatriots he was just Wenceslão Braz.

Parents in Brazil give their children curious first names. Greek and Roman names abound, from the Classics. I had a mulatto porter named Aristotle and a cook called Virgil. Nelson, from the British hero, is common, so are Wilson and Taylor from United States politicians. Incidentally if all the Brazilians who have Cochrane as their first or middle names were direct or even indirect descendants of Lord Cochrane, all I can say is that the British admiral would have had to be as active in Brazilian beds as he was in Brazilian waters.

A Brazilian journalist whom I knew well in Brazil was Assis Chateaubriand. He later became the owner of a chain of Brazilian newspapers and, later still, a senator and Brazilian ambassador in London (1957–59). But he was not a descendant of the author of *Mémoires d'outretombe*. The explanation is that his father admired the French writer. His full name was Assis Chateaubriand Bandeira de Mello. With a certain admiration and affection for this brilliant journalist Brazilians called him Chatô.

Now to return to Benjamin Constant. This is an instance of Brazilian parents being admirers of Benjamin Constant de Rebecque, who was born at Lausanne in 1767, and, before he died in Paris in 1830, seems to have belonged to any political party as it suited him. In Brazilian history Botelho de Magalhães, the man whom the Constituent Assembly proclaimed Founder of the Republic, is known not by that surname, but by his first two names, Benjamin Constant. And that is certainly not on account of any great affection for him. He was a Positivist, and like a large coterie of Brazilians in his day, imbued with the Auguste Comte philosophy. He had served in the Paraguayan War, as had nearly all Brazilian Army officers on the active list in 1889. As a professor at the imperial Military School, Benjamin Constant preached republican philosophy to the cadets.

From the end (June, 1870) of the Paraguayan War onwards, Brazilian army officers considered themselves a caste apart, far above mere civilians, and deserving very special treatment at the hands of the Imperial Cabinet. Deodoro da Fonseca, who "proclaimed" the Republic, was, under the Monarchy, Governor of the province of Rio Grande do Sul. He had come to Rio de Janeiro, not sent for by the Cabinet, but because he had heard that the Prime Minister, dissatisfied with his administration in the southern province and suspecting, rightly, that he was carrying on subversive intrigues in the higher cadres of the Army, contemplated appointing him to command the Imperial garrisons in Mato Grosso, where the immense distance from the coast would itself suffice to keep him out of mischief.

Disgruntled generals can do much mischief, and usually do it. For Colonel Benjamin Constant, who commanded the 2nd Brigade of the Rio de Janeiro garrison, Deodoro da Fonseca's arrival in the capital was a golden opportunity for converting his republican theories into reality. His was the sharper wit. Deodoro should be his tool. When, on November 15, 1889, the latter put himself at the head of Benjamin's Brigade and marched it to the Square facing the palace in which the Imperial Cabinet was meeting, the intention of the Field-Marshal was merely to intimidate the Cabinet. He demanded its resignation. The Prime Minister, Viscount Ouro Preto, refused and called in a colonel of the Household Guard, Floriano Peixoto. This officer had been a corporal when the Paraguayan War began (in 1865) and had risen by merit.

"You will disperse the Military outside," ordered the Prime Minister.

"What with?" said the Colonel ironically.

"I suppose," rejoined the Premier with equal irony, "you have cannon that will shoot."

"Yes," said the Colonel, "but they are all pointing this way—trained on the Palace."

Meanwhile, Deodoro da Fonseca and Benjamin Constant were conversing in the Square, the former telling the latter repeatedly that the Viscount Ouro Preto refused to be intimidated and would not resign.

"So," he said in exasperation, "what can I do now?"

"You have gone too far to draw back now," exclaimed Benjamin Constant exultantly. "There is only one solution, and it will be decisive. You must proclaim the Republic. The troops are ready for anything and will follow you."

Only half-convinced, the Marshal addressed the soldiers telling them that the Cabinet had refused to listen to their just demands. "But I do not take that for an answer. We shall turn this Cabinet out."

The speech was greeted with loud cheers.

"The day is yours," shouted Benjamin Constant into the field-marshal's ear. "Now cry 'Long live the Republic!' "

Carried away by the cheering of the troops, Marshal Deodoro da Fonseca lifted his plumed hat and cried: "Long live the Republic!" And as the cry was taken up with more cheering, the old soldier was heard to mutter in his beard: "And may the devil take it!" Only the word he used for devil was the one attributed to Cambronne.

I tell the story because it is one that was told to me so often when I first went to Brazil by people to whom the declaration of the Republic was as vivid as D-Day is to anybody in England over the age of twenty-two. In 1910 the Brazilian Republic was only twenty years old. The story is told in different ways by Brazilian historians, but the material facts are as I have related them.

I had been posted to Rio de Janeiro of my own choice. Four of us had passed the Consular Exam. and I was given the choice of the four vacant posts: New York, Boston, Baltimore, and Rio de Janeiro. I chose Rio. It sounded much more exciting than the American posts. I was in Belgrade when I made the choice. When I got back to London Lord

Dufferin told me: "We want you to go to Rio de Janeiro as quickly as you can arrange to do so. Casement wants to go on leave and you will take over the Consulate-General from him."

The earliest steamer to leave was German. I booked to go by it. She had a list all the the way out, probably due to badly stowed cargo; but the food was excellent. The ship was full of Germans going out to South America for the first time to jobs in banks and commercial firms. They sat round the decks diligently studying Spanish and Portuguese grammars. At least, that was what they set out to do when they settled down in their deck chairs; but the sun and the good food were too much for them and they were soon asleep. Until Lisbon the decks and the dining-room were nearly empty. I embarked at Dover from a tender—the only passenger, and indeed the only Englishman on board, which was not discovered until the day before we arrived at Rio, except by a German commercial traveller who represented a Dundee firm. We made friends. He had travelled for his firm in South America for many years and I learnt much from my talks with him. In the following years he made a point of looking me up when he passed through Rio.

When I took my ticket at the German shipping company's office in London, the booking clerk enquired whether I was travelling on Goverment service. I asked why he wanted to know. Because, he said, Government officials travelling on German ships were allowed a discount of 15 per cent on the fare.

"Any Government?" I asked.

"Yes," he said.

"In this case," I told him, "the concession will not benefit me personally; but I hope the British Government will be grateful."

Two years later, I went home on leave. I chose the Lamport & Holt *Vandyck* and asked the Rio manager whether the British line would do as the German line had done and allow a discount of 15 per cent. In the present case I should have been the beneficiary, because one paid one's own fares home and back when on leave. There was no discount; indeed, my friend Perkins, the Rio manager, seemed mildly shocked that I should even suggest such a thing. Sixty years ago, British business men were contemptuous of foreign competition. God— English-speaking, of course—was in his Heaven and all was right with the world.

I found Rio de Janeiro very hot and sticky when I landed there in January, 1910. There was only one embassy in Brazil, the United States embassy; all other missions were legations. Our own was in the cool hills of the Organ mountains, at Petropolis, which one reached by stages:— first, a tilbury to a pier-head in Rio to catch a flat-bottomed ferry boat which took one to the northern end of the bay. From there a train took one to the foot of the mountains, where a rack railway climbed the steep slopes to Petropolis. The town had been founded by Emperor Dom Pedro; hence its name. The whole journey took rather more than two hours; but to lose four hours of a working day was of no great importance in the leisurely ways and days of diplomacy. In 1913 the railway came into Rio itself, thus eliminating the ferry-boat journey, its most agreeable stage. By the 1930's a motor road linked Rio de Janeiro to Petropolis.

From November 1 to March 31 is the hot season, when the Rio climate can be very trying, especially at night; but it is by no means intolerable. The reason why the Imperial court and, later, the Republican cabinet did their work in Petropolis was not in order to avoid the heat of Rio but to escape from being bitten by mosquitoes, the transmitters of yellow fever. I was told that yellow fever does not exist in countries where there are no negroes. I do not know how true that is. Early British travellers in Brazil do not mention yellow fever, and the native Indian inhabitants do not appear to suffer from it. Writing in 1877, a Brazilian historian, Dr Moreira de Azevedo, wrote: "In 1850 yellow fever invaded Rio de Janeiro, became acclimatized in our country and has proved fatal to the increase of our population and to the development of our trade and industry."

In 1906, when the first modernization of colonial Rio de

Janeiro was begun, a Brazilian scientist, Dr Oswaldo Cruz, who had studied at the Pasteur Institute and the Toxicological Laboratory in Paris, was given a free hand by the Brazilian authorities to deal with the yellow fever endemic. His problem was both simple and difficult. Mosquitoes breed on the surface of stagnant water and swamps. To spray paraffin periodically on such places would eliminate them as breeding grounds. That was the simple part of the problem. The difficult part was to gain access to the back gardens of private dwellings, where sanitation was elementary. The work of a British enterprise to improve it had only just begun.

Now whether it was a solid Portuguese-built house, or a newer style dwelling, or the humblest log cabin or adobe hut, the Brazilian's house was very much his castle. By tradition, private property was respected, but in the naval revolts, mutinies, and political upsets that had followed the installation of the republic, there had been perquisitions and domiciliary invasions. By 1906 all that was a thing of the past. But the memory of it was vivid, and when Oswaldo Cruz recruited his army of mosquito-killers (*mata-mosquitos*) armed with kerosene tins, to visit every house in Rio and seek permission to disinfect, pour kerosene on stagnant water, and destroy old tins in backyards, there was a howl of popular protest. The whole scheme looked like coming to grief. The Press and the Senate were on the side of the howlers. But the President of the Republic (Rodrigues Alves, from São Paulo) threatened to resign if Oswaldo Cruz were prevented from continuing his work. The threat sufficed, the work went on and was so successful that, as the Brazilian review *A Cigarra* wrote, "his enemies became his warmest advocates."

He was still quite a young man, under 40, when I first met him. He had a shock of white, wavy hair, black moustache and eyebrows: he gave me the impression of a dreamer, despite his reputation as a man of action. Before he died, at the age of 45 during the First World War, he had been Prefect of Petropolis. He was an enthusiast for flowers and Petropolis owes its flower-beds in its squares and streets to him. It was he who introduced hydrangeas to Petropolis, where they flourished exceedingly, so that for Petropolitans they are a flower as symbolic as the lily is to the Florentines.

Our Minister to Brazil, Sir William Haggard, was short and thin. He was fond of relating that he had done "a lot of pig-sticking" in Persia when he was a young Secretary of Legation. He had white wavy hair and whiskers, and into one of his light blue eyes he was constantly sticking a black-rimmed monocle and dropping it. His voice when he was excited, which was often, was an unmusically harsh croak, and he would laugh loudly when telling one of his own stories.

The first time I met him was at dinner at the Legation when I went with Roger Casement to Petropolis to be introduced to him before Casement went on leave, three weeks later. Casement purred away, as was his wont, in his pleasant voice telling about some reception he had attended in Pará, where he had been Consul before being posted to Rio de Janeiro.

"Of course," he was saying, "the foreign consuls, wearing their silly decorations, can always put a British Consul in the shade."

"But you could have worn your CMG," interrupted Haggard. "Why didn't you?"

"Yes, I suppose I could; but I didn't," murmured Casement and relapsed into an almost sulky silence.

Casement had been awarded the decoration five years before. But apparently it gave him a pathological pleasure to nurse grievances, purely imaginary ones, against the British authorities, who, in point of fact, had always rewarded him with exceptional generosity for his services. I saw he had entered his name in the hotel register at Petropolis as *Irish Consul*. When I took over from him at Rio I had to get fresh notepaper printed. Instead of the usual letter-heading British Consulate-General, he had had printed Consulate-General of Great Britain and Ireland. I give him good marks for having retained the Great.

The Legation, which had no residence or chancery in Rio de Janeiro, used a room behind my room (the Consul-General's room) as a *pied à terre* whenever the Minister or a Secretary

came to Rio. One day when Haggard was in my office he
looked at the book-shelf behind my chair for a book of reference. Alongside it was "Memories of My Exile" by Louis
Kossuth.

"I suppose Casement must have left that behind," said
Haggard. "What a queer fellow he is, filling his head with such
revolutionary stuff! If that's the kind of thing he feeds on, no
wonder he's unbalanced."

From my own observation during the month we worked
together at Rio before he went on leave I should diagnose
Casement's case differently. He had a one-way obsession about
Ireland, an obsession amounting to fanaticism. He never
argued on the matter; he never paid the slightest attention to
any argument or objection. He merely waited until the speaker
had stopped—for breath, refreshment, or enlightenment—and
then took up from where he himself had left off, without the
slightest reference to what the other person had refuted or
suggested. England and the English he hated with a positive
hatred. To him the British monarchy was detestable. Yet he
saw nothing incongruous in wearing the King's uniform and
receiving decorations from the King. On the contrary such
things pleased him well, for he was extremely vain.

On all topics, even on Ireland, he was superficial. On many
he was quite ignorant. Imagination he had in plenty, and his
pen flowed as easily as his speech. He might have made
good novelist. Indeed, half the reports he wrote about the
Congo and Putumayo stemmed from his imagination. To say
this, is not to doubt his sincerity; but it was the sincerity of
self-delusion.

Casement took himself far too seriously. There was not
spark of humour in his composition. I never heard him laugh
He was as incapable of amusing as of being amused. The
nearest I ever heard him get to it was one day at lunch at the
City Club at Rio de Janeiro. It was a small luncheon club
which I joined a few days after my arrival. There were
number of small tables, and there was one long table running
the length of the room, in the middle. One day about a dozen
men of heavy build and ponderous demeanour marched in

nd sat down at this table. They talked American, whereas
early all the other members were British, with a sprinkling
f Brazilians.

"What a strange-looking crowd!" I said to Casement.

"That is the Light & Power face," said Casement sardonic-
lly. "They all look the same. They belong to the concern that
uns the electric tramways and supplies electricity."

"But it's a Canadian company, isn't it?" I said.

"Legally, yes," replied Casement. "But it is really American
n thought and deed."

Haggard had used the word "unbalanced" to describe
Casement. It was a word which could at times, not unfairly,
ave been ascribed to Haggard himself. He could be pleasant
nd reasonable; but he was always unaccountable and usually
rritable; at times, he would rave and storm. If his butler,
ewell, did not appear at once in answer to his bell, I have
een Haggard go marching up and down the Legation
orridor, shouting: "Jewell, Jewell, where *is* Jewell, damn the
nan!" And I have looked out of the window and seen Jewell
n the garden, walking towards the house, grinning, and re-
eating like an echo "Jewell, Jewell, damn the man!" A few
noments later he would enter Haggard's study, poker-faced
nd deferential, explaining in reply to Haggard's irate "Where
n earth have you been?" that it was Haggard himself who
ad sent him to the far end of the garden with a message for
ady Haggard.

Lady Haggard was always pleasant and seemed able to
oothe her husband's moods, which, I think, were largely due
o his suffering from rheumatism. Lady Haggard had a well-
rained contralto voice, and at week-ends when I stayed with
hem occasionally, Haggard would get her to sing and me
o play her accompaniments.

In all fairness to Haggard it must be said that the Legation
vas invariably short-staffed. This meant that Haggard had
oo much to do. Like most Haggards, he had the urge to be
vriting. "Put a Haggard alone in a room for half-an-hour with
sheet of foolscap on the table and pen and ink, and at the

95

end of that time he will have covered the sheet." This is how
Reginald Ray put the matter.

Reginald Ray was officially the translator on the Legation
staff. But in reality he was for months on end the only member
of the staff. In his younger days Ray had written a book on
Boadicea. He had lived and worked in Portugal, spoke
Portuguese fluently, and wrote it elegantly. He was short,
broad-shouldered, muscular, and a first-class tennis player.

Dark, with bushy eyebrows over piercing grey eyes, Ray was
at one time during his stay in Portugal a popular figure in the
bullring. Dressed in his tennis flannels he would face a charging
bull, seize the horns and hoist himself into a short-arm balance
until the bull shook him off. This feat delighted the crowd,
which shouted *Viva o Ray! Viv'o Ray!* The pronunciation of
Ray and *Rei* (king) is identical. Dom Carlos was popular with
the masses, though his Government was not. So there was a
double meaning in the cry "*Long live Ray (rei)!*" Dom Carlos
knew all about this and frequently invited Ray to play tennis
with him at Cintra.

In February of 1912 two secretaries did arrive at the Legation: Arnold Robertson, who was Chargé d'Affaires when the
war broke out in 1914; and Stopford Birch. That meant that
Ray was able to go home on leave. In June of that year I
was in England and went to see Ray at his home in Chichester.
I asked him when he was returning to Brazil.

"I am not going back," he told me. "I really could not risk
another long spell of being left alone in the Chancery to put
up with Haggard."

"Have you told the Foreign Office that?" I asked.

"I told them rather more than that," said Ray deliberately.

"What did you tell them then?"

"I told them I refused to go back to Brazil in charge of an
uncertified lunatic."

Haggard had his gay moments and could be an entertaining
host. He was, too, a shrewd observer. Dr Bernardino Machado,
who had been Portuguese Foreign Minister, came to Brazil
as Envoy. Haggard invited him to lunch to meet a few other

96

people. While we were waiting for lunch to be announced the Portuguese Envoy was telling us an interminable story about some incident on the ship that brought him to Brazil. He droned on and on in a low voice and in bad French. (I have never heard so much voluble but badly spoken French as among diplomatists.) Presently Haggard whispered to me: "Keep things going. I want to add something to a despatch of mine that is in the Chancery." Presently he returned. The Portuguese story was still unfinished.

After lunch, when the guests had gone, Haggard said to me: "What a bore the old Portuguese is! Did you know that he had nineteen children?"

"I had heard he had a large family," I said, "but never knew the exact number."

"I drafted my report to the FO this morning on new colleagues," said Haggard, "and told them that the new Portuguese Minister has an exceptionally large family. So when I heard him boring us all with his never-ending story I went to the Chancery and inserted that he was fond of telling dull stories which are as interminable as his progeny seems to be. Pretty good, eh?" And Haggard chuckled with great good humour. This was as characteristic of him as his irritability.

Although Sir William Haggard had spent the greater part of his life in foreign lands, he remained very English and much attached to his native heath, Norfolk and East Anglia. There were in Rio de Janeiro two brothers, Lowndes, both in business on their own account. One of them had been successful in furthering some engineering project dear to the heart of the Emperor Dom Pedro II, who in recognition of what Lowndes had done, created him a Count: Conde de Leopoldina. The Emperor's mother was an Austrian archduchess of that name.

I remember Haggard taking Lowndes to task, pleasantly and almost jocularly, for having been willing, as Haggard put it, "to accept a Brazilian title, when your own family name, English and so well known in England, especially in Essex, is worth so much more."

One of Haggard's amiable traits was that he was very tolerant. He knew all about Casement's foibles, as most people

in the British community did. Haggard merely shrugged his
shoulders when he was told that Casement had signed his name
in the Petropolis hotel register as Irish Consul-General.

People who have written biographies about Casement say
little or nothing at all about his life in Brazil. The explanation
must be that few if any of them knew Casement personally or
had even met him. His features are by now well known to the
public: the dark hair and beard, the swarthy skin, and the
rather sleepy grey eyes. He was tall, sparely made, and a good
swimmer. His voice was soft and insinuating in conversation. I
never heard him raise it. He was a fluent talker and tireless in talking, so that he would out-talk an opponent. He could not argue.

In 1906–08 Casement was Consul at Belém do Pará and
at Santos—in each post for less than a year. He knew nothing
of the hinterland of either place, indeed he knew very little
about Brazil at all. He made no Brazilian friends and had few
English-speaking friends. But, as I have said before, his imagination served him in writing reports. I will quote one instance.

In 1908, when Casement was Consul at Pará, Milne
Cheetham was Chargé d'Affaires at our Legation in Petropolis,
where Reginald Ray was translator. Cheetham was a first-rate
diplomatist, and Ray told me how much he enjoyed working
under him. One day, Cheetham called Ray to his study. He
had before him copy of a copious report that Casement had
sent to the Foreign Office.

"Have you read this?" he asked Ray.

"Not yet," replied Ray. "I have only had time to file it. But
it struck me as interesting when I glanced at it."

"Interesting!" cried Cheetham. "I should just think it was.
Why, it's almost entirely a crib from Wallace's and Bates's
books on the Amazon."

It is doubtful if anybody at the Foreign Office ever spotted
what Cheetham had spotted. If they had, it would probably
not have done Casement any harm. He had always been much
favoured by the FO. Horatio Mackie, who had held Consular
posts in Portuguese West Africa and at Boma shortly after
Casement's time there, passed through Rio de Janeiro in 1911
on his way to take up his appointment as Consul at Buenos

Aires. I asked him whether one could believe all that Casement had written about the conditions he said he found in the Congo, since my experience was that his pen was inclined to run away with him.

"As far as I can make out," Mackie told me, "he didn't visit half the places he says he did; and I know for a fact that he wrote most of the reports sitting comfortably in a well-found river launch at Boma." I could sense that Mackie was not disposed to say more on that topic and that it would be indiscreet to press him. So we talked of Russia, which he knew well, and of Argentina to which he was going for the first time.

George Beak, who succeeded me as Consul at Bâle in 1916 and who had been one of "H.M. Vice-Consuls in the Independent State of the Congo" in 1907–11, confirmed to me what Mackie had hinted at. So did Gerald Campbell, with whom I served for a short time at Venice in 1914. He, too, had served in the Congo—from 1908 to 1913—and deplored the sensationalism of so much that was written and believed about the Congo. He instanced Conan Doyle's "Congo Atrocities" pamphlet, which was apparently based on Casement's reports. The pamphlet had a cover depicting a negro boy with one hand missing. The boy lived in the Kasai district and when Campbell visited it in the course of his Consular duties he found the boy and asked him how he had lost his hand. "A leopard bit it off," was the reply.

I heard much the same kind of comment on Casement's "Putumayo atrocities" reports when I visited Amazonia in 1916. One was about a Barbadian cook, whose missing hand was reported as an atrocity, whereas the man had lost it in a sugar-grinding machine.

Here is a glimpse of Casement as told by one who knew him personally in Brazil. Charles Good, to whom I refer, was representative of the Booth Line and other important British interests in the Amazon valley for over fifty years. He had an unrivalled knowledge of the region and of everybody and everything in it or connected with it. A few years ago, when there was much ado in British newspapers about Casement and his Diaries, Good wrote this to me:— "Roger Casement

99

came to Pará to take up his appointment as Consul early in 1908, and lived with us for the first few weeks while he was looking for independent quarters. We soon got tired of him, on account of his fanaticism on everything concerning the Emerald Isle.

"You may remember, by the way, that in the Consular Report he wrote when he was Consul at Santos he included the Royal Mail steamer *Araguaya* not among 'British exports to Brazil,' but separately as an import from Ireland!!

"The last I saw of Casement was one day in 1913 when he turned up at our Adelphi Terrace office trailing with him a couple of black Barbadians he had brought back from the Putumayo to support his statements about the atrocities there. I wonder whether, if today any similar allegations were made about goings-on in a foreign country, we could get an interested and indirectly accused party to come to England and give evidence like old Julio Araña did.* I am afraid that if we as much as hinted at it, we should be told to go to hell. Old Julio Araña showed up very well at that enquiry.

"By the way, in 1925 I was a fellow passenger to the Amazon with Lord Athlumney who was Governor of the Tower when Casement was held there, after he gave himself up in Ireland. Incidentally, I read Shane Leslie's letter to the 'Daily Telegraph' and noticed his reference to your work."**

Had Casement not been afflicted with the *cacoethes scribendi* there would have been no diaries, though it was not the diaries which brought him to the scaffold, as some writers seem to imply. It was a tragic end for a man who had great charm, but whose inordinate vanity made him deplorably stupid. From what he himself told me when we met again in England

---

*Araña was the manager of the Peruvian company against which atrocities in the Putumayo rubber collecting zone were alleged. These charges Araña refuted. In any case, it seems obvious that one cannot commit atrocities and retain labourers to collect rubber. That would be self-defeating.

**The letter referred to was dated April 21, 1956. In it Sir Shane Leslie wrote: "As hundreds of pens are rushing into print, I would ask why it is impossible to get the only book published by a colleague of Casement—*British Consul* by Ernest Hambloch, 1938."

in 1912, it was obvious (except to him) that the Germans were making a tool of him. When war came, they soon discovered how shallow his pretensions were and landed him in Ireland to pay the penalty of being of no use to them. They had their own ways of getting rid of people who wasted their time by failing to deliver the goods.

In the *Münchner Neueste Nachrichten* of May 29, 1915, which among other war news reports a Zeppelin bomb-dropping attack on Southend, an "Interview with Sir Roger Casement" occupies two columns. He had been spending a week in Munich and was questioned on "the Findlay Incident". The British Minister in Christiana, Mansfeldt de Cardonnel Findlay, was reported as having promised £5,000 to Casement's valet, Adler Christensen, "to deliver his master to the English Government."

The Norwegian Government, says the Munich newspaper, could do nothing about "these criminal plots, because they took place in the British Legation and therefore in a sense on British soil". Sir Edward Grey had "not had the courage to refute the charge of incitement to assassination."

The German newspaper went on to report that, according to Casement, "Irish enthusiasm in the United States is for Germany and peace, but only with Germany as the victor."

There was a lot about Ireland in the Munich paper's article which said that the Leader of an Irish Delegation that had visited Paris at the end of April was not Irish at all, but "an English journalist, O'Connor, who represents Liverpool in the House of Commons". The interview closed with a statement of Casement's conviction that the Irish were "in favour of establishing the secular power of the Pope and settling the 'Romish question'."

On September 18, 1914, the same paper had reported declarations by Casement to the American Associated Press, saying that his "sympathies belong to Germany," and that "Germany did not wish to fight."

Chapter VII

The British in Brazil — A Brazilian Aeneas — Some diplomatists — At Lowther Castle — A Consular rescue job — Some Americans in Brazil and London — The diamond expert from South Africa — The Australian clairvoyant — An incident with Casement — The Head of the Civil Service? — The Marconi Scandal — Getting run over for a pension — Street names.

THE DEATH of King Edward VII in May, 1910, only a few weeks after my arrival in Rio de Janeiro, brought home to me two things: first, that as Acting Consul-General I was officially head of the British community there; and secondly, that there was no British official centre in Rio or indeed anywhere in Brazil. There were clubs, some social but mostly sporting; and there were benevolent organizations. But there was nothing national. Nor did British firms possess any representative commerical entity. When I left Brazil at the end of my four years' spell as Acting Consul-General, I made up my mind that if ever I returned to Brazil in an official capacity I would try and rectify what I considered deficiencies: the one social, the other commercial. In the latter case I was successful; in the former I failed, as will be seen later on.

When we knew of King Edward's death my immediate concern was to get representatives of the British community together, in order to decide what form "loyal expression of regret" should take. Similarly, in the following year, we had to decide how to celebrate the coronation of King George V. The only way of reaching the business community was by advertising in the leading local newspaper, the *Jornal do Commercio*. At the City Club and other clubs, too, I was able to consult heads of British firms; and there was the padre, Graham, a tower of strength and the best of good fellows, an ex-Indian army chaplain.

No locally produced British newspaper circulated in Brazil. There had been one, an influential organ published by Scully, a British resident who enjoyed the Emperor's confidence; but when Scully died, his paper died too. There were to be others later on; but in 1910 there was only one publication in English, a financial weekly named after its owner and editor "Wileman's Review". It was written for consumption in the City of London.

The militarily moustached padre who ran the Anglican Church, the Rev. John Graham, was an accomplished musician. No consul could have wished for a more co-operative padre than Graham in the delicate and sometimes complicated questions relating to marriages in which one of the parties was a British subject.

Two other British institutions deserve mention. One was the English library, housed modestly over a boot shop in the rua do Ouvidor, Rio's shady shopping street. It was looked after by an old German, Strube by name, who had fought with the Brazilian Army in the Paraguayan War of 1865–70.

The other institution was the British cemetery. This had historical origins. One of the first acts of the Prince Regent, Dom João, on his arrival in Rio with the Portuguese royal family in 1808, was to incorporate into the Crown patrimony a small landed property with a foreshore on the bay. The property was already serving as a burial ground for British and other non-Catholic residents in Rio de Janeiro. It was in the Gamboa district of Rio, and the crews of British sailing ships, victims of yellow fever, could be conveniently rowed to the cemetery for burial there. The land belonged to a certain Simon Martins de Castro. The Prince Regent paid him the equivalent in those days of £500 for it. Then, by clause 12 of the Treaty of Trade and Navigation, signed by the Brazilian minister, Count Linhares, and the British envoy, Lord Strangford, on February 19, 1810, Brazil donated this country property to serve as the "last resting place for the subjects of the Very High and Very Mighty King of the United Kingdom of Great Britain and Ireland."

In June, 1911, when King George V was crowned, our

Chargé d'Affaires at Rio de Janeiro was William O'Reilly. It fell to me to make the arrangements for an official banquet given by the British community to the Brazilian authorities to mark the event. The banquet took place at the Club of the Daily Ones (*Club dos Diarios*), as no British club was large enough for such an occasion. The name of the club is somewhat unusual. It had been founded in Imperial and yellow-fever days by high Government officials and heads of firms who made the *daily* journey from Petropolis to Rio de Janeiro, where they had leisure to lunch, play poker, or read the papers. Even in 1910 restaurants in Rio were still primitive.

It was at the Coronation banquet that I had my first experience of Brazilian oratory.

In proposing the loyal toast O'Reilly read a short speech referring to the responsibilities of a constitutional monarch. Then followed the customary toast to the President of the Republic, to which Senhor Eneas Martins, the Under-Secretary for Foreign Affaires, replied. He was a dark, round-faced little man from Pará, for which he had been Federal deputy and of which he would later on be Governor. He had been a close collaborator of the famous Foreign Minister, Baron do Rio Branco, and had signed the Putumayo navigation agreement with Colombia at Bogotá. I got to know him quite well. He pooh-poohed what he called "Casement's Putumayo atrocity stories."

My schoolboy recollection of "pious Aeneas" was that he was a considerable bore. But this eloquent Brazilian Aeneas was precisely the reverse. He spoke for twenty minutes without notes of any kind, emphasizing the part played by the British in Brazil's struggle for independence. He pointed out how the principle of constitutional monarchy in Brazil was akin to that in Great Britain—all this and more in the well-rounded, well constructed phrases to which the Portuguese language lends itself in the hands of a skilful manipulator. In other hands its prose is often stodgy and its oratory bombastic.

Some months later I was sitting next to Eneas Martins in the lounge of a German steamer anchored in the bay. We had each been to see friends off to Europe.

"They do things very well on these boats, and the food is very good," he said to me.

"I travelled out on one," I told him. "But wasn't comfortable. The ship had a bad list."

"Still, that must be unusual," he said.

"Do you prefer travelling by German ships?" I asked him.

"For food, yes, I should prefer it," replied Eneas Martins. "But for safety I choose British—the Royal Mail or the Booth Line ships."

There is no doubt that in the early 1900's British enterprises were well dug in throughout Brazil. Merchant houses, banks (there were three of them), insurance companies, railways, shipping lines, public utilities—some of them could even then claim to have been operating in Brazil for over a century. Today the situation is rather different. During the First World War the Americans began to "come down like the wolf on the fold". But that is not the only difference. The British have been middle class and class conscious. Other European immigrants to Brazil have not suffered from those inhibitions. Many Britons have become domiciled in Brazil. Few have been settlers.

O'Reilly of our Legation and von Egger, the Austrian Chargé d'Affaires, were great friends. Their wives were contrasting beauties. Mrs O'Reilly was a blue-eyed blonde, extremely intelligent, the daughter of a one-time *Hofmarschall* at the Court of Berlin. Madame von Egger, an Englishwoman, was a tall, *svelte* brunette, with soft dark eyes and an engaging manner. Mrs O'Reilly talked perfect English; so did von Egger. O'Reilly spoke German quite well; Mme von Egger not at all. They were all four frequently together. I could see that von Egger was a great admirer of Mrs O'Reilly, while O'Reilly made no secret to me of his admiration for Mme von Egger. This *partie carée* was amusing to watch. But when war came, O'Reilly found himself in a backwater at the Foreign Office because there were few posts abroad to which he could be sent owing to his wife's being German by birth.

By the same token Mme von Egger found herself awkwardly placed as the English-born wife of an enemy diplomatist. In August, 1914, while I was still at Ragusa (Dubrovnik) and just after Austria had declared war on Serbia and Montenegro, I met von Egger again. He was passing through on his way to Vienna from Cetinje where he had been Austrian Minister. He seemed much depressed. I asked after his wife. He told me she was in London. "I may join up when I get to Vienna," he told me. I think he might have preferred army life to the diplomatic service. In any case, like Count Bernhard von Bülow, the German ambassador in Rome, he certainly preferred army uniform to diplomatic uniform, for at the Service which we arranged at the Anglican Church at Rio de Janeiro to celebrate King George V's coronation and which was attended by the foreign diplomatic corps, von Egger, representing Austria, turned up in a resplendent military uniform with plumed helmet, sword and spurs.

By charm of manner and immense self-assurance O'Reilly was a born diplomatist, and with those qualities he combined a keen and quick perception none too common in those that are sent to "lie abroad for the good of their country." But by temperament he was an inventor, and, to Mrs O'Reilly's chagrin, quite unambitious in his profession. The model of a three-masted schooner stood on his sideboard when I dined with them while spending a few days in London during the First World War. He had made it entirely himself. When I admired it, Mrs O'Reilly remarked with a wry smile: "He might have employed his time better ingratiating himself with the dispensers of favour in the Foreign Office!" O'Reilly took the comment in good part, and we went on to talk about Bulgaria, which had been his last post.

When I went home on leave in 1912 I took with me a collection of Indian bows and arrows from Mato Grosso— much to my mother's alarm, since the tops of the arrows were believed to be poisoned and the bows spanned over 7 ft. Where was she to put them? I consoled her by telling her that Lord Lonsdale had taken a fancy to them. I had met him in Rio de Janeiro on his way to Buenos Aires to open the first

Argentine Horse Show and entertained Lady Lonsdale and him during their short stay in Rio. I stayed a few days with them at Lowther Castle, where he had quite a museum of objects connected with hunting. His library was devoid of interest. The baronial castle built for the Lowther family by Robert Smithe in the 1850's was cold, gloomy, and vast. To live there was like living in a cathedral. But the hospitality of the Lonsdales was unbounded.

I think Lonsdale, the 5th earl, was flattered to have been invited by the German Kaiser some years before to assist at German army manoeuvres. He showed me some photos of the occasion. There was a signed photograph of Dom Manoel, the exiled King of Portugal, in one of the rooms.

"Yes," said Lord Lonsdale in reply to my question. "He came and stayed with us for the shooting."

"Does he hope to be restored to the throne one day?" I asked.

"I shouldn't wonder," replied Lonsdale. "But I have the impression that he is quite happy as he is. No worries."

"Apparently not even money worries. I wonder where kings in exile get their money from. I don't think Daudet ever made that point clear in his novel about kings in exile." But I saw that the allusion was lost on Lord Lonsdale, who merely shrugged his shoulders.

Colonel Charles Repington, the famous *Times* military critic in the First World War, described in his reminiscences how on rising from the table after dinner at Lowther Castle large dogs, whose presence one had never suspected, would emerge from the dark corners of the room and await a word of command from their master.

Another foible of Lord Lonsdale's was that he and all his keepers should be dressed exactly alike out of doors. He told me with great glee how a German had called at the Castle one day. Lonsdale was out shooting, but had left instructions that the visitor, whom he expected, should be directed to some place on the estate where he would meet the game-keepers, who could tell him where to find Lord Lonsdale. The latter, acting the part of head game-keeper, told the German they must all sit down and wait for milord. The German soon began asking indiscreet questions about Lord Lonsdale, his habits, his reputed wealth, and so on. At the end of fifteen minutes the German, struck by the involuntary deference shown to Lord Lonsdale by the others, tumbled to the fact that he had been hoaxed. Lord Lonsdale related all this to me with boyish glee. Indeed, it seemed to me that there was much of the schoolboy in his idea of fun.

He told me he got his famous long cigars direct from Germany. I was at a luncheon party he gave at the Olympia when he was the presiding genius at one of the Shows there. When the cigars were handed round, a foreign diplomatist, one of the guests, turned to Lord Lonsdale and said: "A big cigar, indeed, milord. It reminds me of the occasion when King Edward gave a foreign guest one of his cigars. The guest was so overcome by the honour that he exclaimed: 'Your Majesty, I will smoke this cigar all my life'."

Lord Lonsdale spoke with enthusiasm about the farms he had visited in Argentina. At one of them, he told me, "they rounded up more prize bulls for me to see than the Duke of Portland has ever owned. They ride well, do the *gaúchos;* but they use too much spur."

"But you use spurs, too, when you ride, don't you?" I said.

"I wear them, because it is part of one's riding kit. But there are no rowels in my spurs; just a little revolving disk."

"And if you want to urge on your mount?"

"Hands and knees are all you need to convey your message to your horse," he said.

Years later, when I spent some time up country in Brazil, I remembered what he told me, and never wore spurs. But I am a poor rider, and mostly rode mules—patient, sure-footed animals. Nor did I often have to ride fast, except once in Minas Gerais when I was with half-a-dozen other men. They started to gallop and my mule joined in without urging from me.

Not infrequently a Consul is called upon to rescue a compatriot from the consequences of his own imprudence. Seamen from British ships in a foreign port are British subjects, whatever their nationality. Common cases of misbehaviour are connected with drink or women or both. The Rio de Janeiro police used to be very tolerant, and more often than not would release a man next morning when he had sobered up. In which case I would not know anything about it officially. Or they would consult me over the telephone. Occasionally, I would have to go to the police station in the Red Lamp district and give guarantees for the wrong-doer.

On one occasion I was asked to call on the Chief of Police himself. He wanted to talk to me about a person they had arrested the night before. It happened that I had crossed swords with this official over a coal cargo in a British ship, and as I had had the better of the argument, I wondered if he would be hostile. But when I was shown into his office he received me very politely. We had not met personally. Our duel had been in writing. He was an olive-skinned, dark-haired man from the north-east of Brazil, the drought zone. He was gigantically built, which is rare in people from that district, but what struck me particularly when he rose to greet me was the inordinate length of his arms which seemed to reach down to below his knees. But nothing could exceed the courtesy of Senhor Belisário Távora. Having invited me to take a chair beside him at his very large desk, he explained that an Englishman had been arrested the night before during a fracas in a brothel. He had evidently had too much to drink.

"Your police inspectors in the district are usually very understanding about such matters," I said.

"Yes, but there is something else in this case," said the Chief of Police.

It appeared that the police who had made the arrest had reason to suspect that the Englishman was engaged in what the Brazilians call *lenocínio*, or the trade of pimping, which in England is usually called, rather portentously, White Slave Traffic. This unexpected turn surprised me. I knew the man by name. He worked on his own as a commercial agent and had the reputation of a keen man of business.

"If you can vouch personally for his honesty and decency,"

the Chief of Police was saying, "then I shall assume that the denunciation made against him is false and malicious."

"I think I can give you the assurance you want," I said. "But I think I ought to see him."

Távora rang a bell and gave an order. In a few moments a rather dishevelled British subject was admitted and told to sit down. I asked permission to speak to him in English. The Chief of Police nodded assent.

"I think you know me," I told my erring business man, "though we have never met." He nodded. "Have you heard what they are saying about you—what you are being accused of?" He nodded again. "Good. Now see if you can explain matters to the Chief of Police."

Upon which my "distressed British subject" did so in quite good Portuguese. There had been a row with another man over women and so on.

"I am quite prepared to accept the explanation," said Belisário Távora. He rang a bell and told the orderly: "This gentleman can go."

I stayed for a few moments to thank the Chief of Police for his consideration. We exchanged a few compliments and parted good friends.

When I got outside I found my compatriot waiting to thank me. I congratulated him on his fluency in Portuguese. He smiled wryly and said: "I expect the trouble last night was that I was *too* fluent in some of the compliments I flung around. But quite seriously, one must learn the language if one hopes to do business in this country." Within a few years he was one of the leading men in the British commerical community. But there is more to it than language. Patience and persistence are equally necessary.

Compared with the British and other European nations, the Americans, though the largest buyers of Brazil's major export, coffee, were late-comers to business in Brazil. The Standard Oil Company, for instance, though sending its products to Brazil through agents who happened to be British, did not open offices and depots of their own in Brazil until 1910. The man they sent out to do this was James Woltman, an American of German Lutheran stock. His wife was English. He had travelled a great deal for his firm and knew South Africa well. We lived in the same French pension on the Santa Thereza hill. One day I was extolling Campbell-Bannerman's policy in having granted virtual independence to the Transvaal and the Orange River Colony so soon after the Boer War.

"Then why on earth did your people ever fight the war!" was Woltman's dry comment.

I took him up on this, for I was a keen Liberal in those days. I pointed out to Woltman that Campbell-Bannerman had always strenuously opposed the war, even at the risk of losing the leadership of the Liberal party.

Curiously enough, Woltman, tolerant in most things and of an imperturbable calm at all times, was at heart an imperialist. I have, indeed, found that this is the case with most educated Americans, and I imagine Woltman voiced their opinion in a conversation we had fifty years ago. In one of our many discussions about world affairs, there had been a reference to British warships, showing the flag, in Chinese waters.

"But your people should let *us* do all that," said Woltman.

"Why mustn't *we*? Has Washington got some sort of prior lien on China?" I scoffed.

"In a way, yes," said Woltman quite seriously. "You see, we are a Pacific Power. You are not. Our west coast faces Asia's east coast. We must protect our Pacific coast; so China and the Pacific are our affair, not yours."

A really interesting American was John Gordon, whose ancestry was Scottish, as his name implies. He, too, had married an English wife. By profession Gordon was a mining engineer. And he had wielded pick-axe and shovel in a mine after leaving the University.

Gordon had come to Brazil in the days of the monarchy and met his wife in Rio de Janeiro. He had done coffee business in Brazil, among other things. He was a prodigious walker, and I never met a man of greater energy. We used to go long Sunday walks together climbing some of the hills round Rio.

In one of his excursions some years before I knew him, he saw something in the composition of the sand along the sea shore to the north of Rio de Janeiro which attracted his attention. He collected a quantity of it and took it back with him for analysis in his laboratory. "I am sure the stinks and occasional explosions in my lab. convinced my Brazilian servants that I was in league with the devil," Gordon told me. "That was back in the 1880's. They certainly thought I was mad, for one day I called my gardener, who didn't hear me, and the cook, apparently not thinking I could hear her, shouted: '*O José, o maluco está chamando!*' (Joe, the lunatic is calling!)"

The sand that Gordon collected from the Brazilian beaches and analysed proved to be monazite. His fortune was made, but not until after many difficulties with State and Federal authorities. The story he told me was this. "I walked into the offices of the Welsbach Company at Vienna. When I told them I could supply them with cheaper and larger quantities of thorium for their incandescent lamps than what they were buying anywhere else, we fixed up our contracts, and that was that."

Twenty years later xenophobia had succeeded in clamping down on the exportation of monazite from Brazil. The gainers were those interested in Travancore deposits. But Gordon was still a very rich man when I knew him. Tall, lean, athletic, he was always fit; but never made a fetish of being so. We lived in the same pension. He loved his game of bridge. If he could not get it, one would probably find him in his room reading Josephus.

I asked him one day—he was then about 65—if he had never thought of retiring. "I did retire once," he said. "I did the social round with my wife, who loves it. You know, the London season, the cure at some continental spa, shooting in Scotland, balls, operas, the whole outfit. But at the end of two years I could stand it no more."

"So you went into harness again?" I said.

"Yes," he said smiling. "I resumed the chase of the nimble dollar."

"You meet all sorts of people when you are in London," I said to Gordon one day. "Can you explain why it is that the critics at home, even when they praise anything of Kipling's, seem to do so grudgingly?"

"The reason is quite simple," said Gordon. "Kipling is not one of theirs. He got into literature by the back door."

"How so," I exclaimed, "by the back door?"

"What I mean is that he didn't come in through Fleet Street, or with an Oxford or Cambridge background. He suddenly appeared as a young and popular author whom they, the critics, had not analyzed, approved of, or pushed. In many cases they may not even have heard of him. As I say, he is not one of theirs. By back door I mean India, and for the lordly London critics that was rather worse than provincial."

"But there are exceptions to that," I said. "Men like Wells, Arnold Bennett, and Barrie."

"Yes, but they were at least filtered, so to say, in Fleet Street," said Gordon. "They belong. Kipling, on the other hand, is an outsider. He had no business to be successful without their prior sanction. The London critics will never *fully* accept him. Besides, the man has genius—an unpardonable sin."

"Why?" I asked, amused.

"Because", replied Gordon, "the critics can neither account for his genius, nor ignore it."

When Caruso came to Rio de Janeiro in 1917 he sang the name part in Carlos Gomes's "national" opera *Guarani* with great success. Some friends of mine invited me to join them, Caruso would be of the party, and they would go for a drive after sunset. We went by the motor road that leads to Tijuca. Half way up there is a gap in the thick forest foliage, through which one had a superb view of Rio. There we got out. It was quite dark, and the myriad lights of the city twinkled like stars against the black drop curtain of a theatre. The view was so impressive that no one spoke. Suddenly Caruso began singing *E lucevan le stelle*. . . I never hear the third act of *Tosca* now without recalling that unique occasion. Caruso's magnificent

H

voice echoing in the dark stillness of a tropical forest. Having sung *e muoio disperato*! Caruso turned to us with a jest, and we all came back to earth.

During my few months' leave in 1912 I spent much of my time with my mother and sister in London. They were then staying at the Pembridge Court Hotel. The room I occupied was to be the scene, forty years later, of one of the most sadistic murders ever recorded—the Heath affair. Fortunately coming events do not always cast their shadow before them, at any rate not so far ahead! In 1912 all was peace, plenty, and respectability.

Among the guests were a Mr and Mrs Vanosten and their small daughter from South Africa. He was friendly, but not talkative. All that the proprietress knew about him was contained in two words: Kimberley, Diamonds. When my mother and sister went to South Africa in 1914 they and the Vanostens became great friends. It appears that Vanosten, even when a boy, possessed the gift of being able to identify the place of origin of any uncut diamond shown to him. This power is innate and cannot be acquired, say those who know; and few people have the gift.

Brazil is, of course, as much a diamond country as South Africa, and the blue-tinted Brazilian diamond is more beautiful than its yellow-tinted South African rival. But if in human relationship kissing goes by favour, preference in business goes by finance; and so the South African diamond ranks higher than the Brazilian in the estimation of the experts, though not in that of all women. Be that as it may, we had often heard that diamonds could be picked up on the seashore along the west coast of Africa, or rather could have been, if one could have got permission to go there.

In Brazil I had heard stories of "pudding basins of cut diamonds" being brought up from bank vaults at the Cape and shown to privileged persons. It was said, too, that if all the cut diamonds thus stored were "released" to the world, these precious stones would no longer be precious. When I returned to Brazil I passed these stories on to my sister in

South Africa. In reply my sister wrote to me: "Mother and I met the Vanostens again recently when we were on holiday at the Cape. They are now living in Cape Town. I didn't mention pudding basins to Mr Vanosten, but I did allude to what you said about 'diamonds kept in bank vaults'. As you will remember, he is not talkative; but he smiled, and invited us to visit him at his office the next day. We did so. But before being admitted we were surveyed by officials through a grille let into the door: a strange experience. Inside his office he showed us, arranged on pieces of blotting paper and laid out on a long table, pieces of rough-looking stones—nothing like the cut diamond. These were diamonds from various mines in various districts.

"He then told us about masses of stones which could be picked up at places along the seashore at Orangemouth, and how the natives there soon learned which were the places and could recognize the stones. These they then smuggled in a number of most original ways out of the country."

In Brazil, at the Morro Velho gold mine in Minas Gerais, then a British enterprise, I have seen old negro women seated at a very slowly revolving round stone table on to which lumps of ore from the mine were fed by a hopper. These lumps they examined, choosing some, which were placed aside, and rejecting others. The chosen ones contained ore veins. I asked the mine manager whether chemical analysis in their well-equipped laboratory would not be a more scientific way of doing this separation.

"We are always checking and analysing," he told me. "But these women, we find, never make a mistake."

To revert to my sister's letter. "Naturally," she wrote, "mines, both gold and silver, are a great asset to this country's economy, and laws against illicit diamond buying are very severe—*almost* the death penalty, I believe! We had heard about IDB, of course, but never fully realized what the letters implied. Vanosten told us that diamonds are to be picked up almost by the basinful, if you know where to look. Which confirms what you heard in Brazil."

Later, during the First World War, my sister returned to the subject in a letter to me. She was writing about the military success of Botha and Smuts in German South-West Africa. "We hear many stories from men who have served with them there," she wrote, "more especially about the way the Germans have treated the native Hereros, a worthy tribe, whom they have almost wiped out. In Potchefstroom one of my 'Dutch' staff married a German farmer, who before the war owned a huge ranch in Lüderitzland, and whenever she came on holiday to see us we used to hear more tales about some of these Germans. It is, my geologist friends tell me, a so-called fault in the soil structure which causes this 'escape' of diamonds to German South-West Africa."

Some years ago, my sister showed me a letter she had received from friends of hers in South Africa. They wrote: "We hear about Russian ships being sent to fish off Angra Pequena. Orangemouth is now like a besieged town, surrounded by barbed wire and high walls, but with every possible amenity within those walls—at least, so we are told."

At the little hotel in Pembridge Gardens in 1912 were some Australians, with whom we made friends: a Mr Wilding, his wife, mother and a sister. He wanted to "do" Great Britain thoroughly by car, and with his motoring map we would try and work out a tour which should miss out nothing and yet not be too tiring. They were due to start their tour a few days after my impending departure for Brazil. The ladies often spoke of a Miss Laker, a clairvoyant, whom the Wildings had known in Australia. She had just arrived in London. I was interested to see how keen Wilding was to help her get a connexion and do well. I asked him why. He told me he had unbounded faith in her gift of clairvoyance and indeed of prediction. That was understandable. A few years earlier, he had been earning his living as a clerk in an insurance office in Sydney. One day, in the lunch hour, he was walking down the street with a companion, when they noticed a new sign which read: Madame Laker, clairvoyant. Consultations 2/6. "We decided to spring 2/6 for a lark," Wilding told me. "She didn't tell my pal much, for he came out regretting his half-crown."

"What does she use?" I asked. "A crystal ball, or cards, or what?"

"Nothing at all," said Wilding; "and that is the astonishing part. She sat in a room in which the only furniture was a table and a few chairs. A curtain across the window kept the room in semi-darkness. I sat opposite her and I put my hand in hers across the table. She closed her eyes and said nothing for some moments. Then she told me I was fond of sport, was easy-going, had no artistic taste. All of which is true. Then she said suddenly: 'In a short time you will be a rich man.' At which I laughed. I told her I was an insurance clerk, with no prospects of getting rich. All she said was: 'That is what the voices tell me.' "

"And did you make a quick fortune, after all?" I asked.

"Not exactly," replied Wilding. "What happened was that I was left a legacy by an uncle here in England of whose existence I was hardly aware."

Wilding was insistent that we should all go and have our fortunes told in a flat he had engaged for her in the West end. A tall man in evening dress under a light overcoat stood in the doorway of the block of flats. He was staring into vacancy but automatically stood aside for us to pass. "That", I whispered, "was Lord Kitchener. Perhaps he has been to consult Madame Laker."

We sat in the drawing-room while the ladies trooped in one after the other to a smaller room to be interviewed by Madame Laker. My sister was not easily impressionable, but when she came out from her interview she whispered to me while the others were talking: "Do you know that Madame Laker described papa to me exactly—his dark wavy hair and reddish brown moustache, and she said he had a slight impediment in his speech." That was indeed curious. My father had been dead twenty years, and the clairvoyant had never seen any of us before: did not know of our existence. My father did have a faint stutter when he was excited.

Wilding insisted that I, too, consult the oracle, despite my protests that I was the most sceptical person in the world. However, I thought it would be ill-mannered if I persisted in refusing, so in I went. In the darkened room were a table and a few chairs, exactly as Wilding had described the setting in Australia. She took my hand, and after some moments said I did not live in England. She thought I was a writer.

"Not exactly," I told her, "though I do have to write a great deal."

"I'm afraid that is all I can tell you," she said smiling. She was a well-spoken women, quiet and unaffected.

We rejoined the others in the drawing-room where coffee was being served. Wilding drew me aside. "Are you satisfied?" he asked.

"I am pleased to have met Madame Laker," I said. "But she really did not tell me anything."

"Madame Laker," he said, approaching her. "Mr Hambloch says he is not satisfied." I protested I had said no such thing.

"Come in and see me again when we have finished coffee," said Madame Laker. I deprecated bothering her again, but she and Wilding both insisted.

"You know," she said, when we were seated, "I can feel you are not psychic. But try and not oppose. Try to want to hear something from me." That seemed fair enough. This time she did not ask to hold my hand. She merely closed her eyes. After a little while she began to describe Rio de Janeiro, without naming it, told me I had a busy and varied life in which ships played some part. "I think you come from Peru. That's all I can tell you. You're not psychic." She opened her eyes when she said that. There was no difference in her tone of speaking as a clairvoyant or in ordinary conversation.

"May I ask you something about yourself?" I said to her. She nodded acquiescence. "This faculty of divination that you possess—how did you acquire it?"

"I did not acquire it at all," said Madame Laker. "I merely repeat what the Voices tell me."

"What are these Voices, as you call them?"

"I don't know," she said. "I have always heard them ever since I was a girl. During my few years of marriage I still heard them. Then my husband died unexpectedly, leaving me quite

118

unprovided for, so I thought I could earn my living as a clairvoyant. And that's how I met Mr Wilding."

We rejoined the others who crowded round her. I thanked Wilding for a very interesting experience. Then I said to him: "I notice you are the only one who has not consulted Madame Laker this evening. Aren't you curious to know still more?"

"Oh yes," he replied smiling. "I have often asked her to tell me more. But she won't. Says she has told me quite enough. I certainly can't complain at what she did tell me!"

When I left for Brazil a few days later, the Vanostens had gone back to South Africa and the Wildings were making their final preparations for their much-planned motor tour in England and Scotland. The very first letter I received from my sister after my arrival in Rio de Janeiro told me that Wilding had been knocked down by a bus in Oxford Street and killed.

Before I returned to Brazil Lord Dufferin had seen to it that I should receive the full office allowance allocated to the Consulate-General. Until then, nearly half of it had gone into Casement's pocket. Pullen, the shipping clerk, was grossly underpaid, and the only other assistance I had was an occasional part-time clerk. Casement's young Portuguese protégé in the office received a salary, but was quite illiterate. Between them, these people absorbed only half the office allowance. The balance went into Casement's pocket, so that I was desperately overworked. By having the whole office allowance at my disposal for the next two years I was able to staff the office properly. And I got rid of Casement's protégé.

While I was working in the Foreign Office a question came up: Who was the "Head of the Civil Service"? (Sir) Algernon Law, who was Controller of Commercial and Consular Affairs at the Foreign Office and had represented the Government at many international conferences, was most emphatic that there was no such animal. Indeed, he was very angry. The question, he said, seemed to crop up periodically. It was usually someone in the Treasury who had some interest in starting the hare. Law's view on the matter was quite positive

and, I think, unanswerable. It was this:—Every Prime
Minister is *ex officio* First Lord of the Treasury. But that does
not automatically confer on the senior civil servant in the
Treasury precedence over every other senior civil servant in
every other Government department. The Permanent Under-
secretaries of the various ministries are responsible to their
respective Ministers (or Secretaries of State). Each was senior
in his own sphere. All are colleagues, and there is no hierarchical rule laid down anywhere by which one of these
permanent officials becomes or should be considered Head of
the Civil Service.

Law, a small, dark-haired, dapper little man, who always
had a monocle in reserve for occasions like this, was at his most
caustic on the subject. And he could be very caustic indeed. I
wish I could have heard what he must have said when in those
three fateful years from May 1937 to May 1940 Sir Horace
Wilson, Permanent Secretary at the Treasury, became Neville
Chamberlain's Grand Vizier, and not only ran the Treasury
but overran the Permanent Under-Secretary at the Foreign
Office and was proclaimed *urbi et orbi* Head of the Civil
Service, being apparently *de facto* Keeper of the Prime
Minister's conscience.

It is difficult for British residents in a foreign country, and
doubly difficult for British officials there, to explain or rather
explain away happenings at home that amount to scandals.
Social scandals do not matter. Every country has them. Everybody understands them. Indeed, they are welcome fuel for
gossip. It is when the scandal is political or financial, or both,
that explanations are unconvincing and excuses damning.

The Marconi scandal of 1912–13 made one feel peculiarly
uncomfortable, for the scandal was both financial and political,
and was made worse by the cover-up tactics employed at home.
Why commentators, considering the case after the lapse of
half-a-century, should accuse those who brought the affair to
light of being "virulent anti-Semitic Right-wing journalists"
or refer to men like Belloc and Chesterton as having been
engaged in "gutter writings" is passing strange. Would they

stigmatize Zola and Clemenceau as Left-wing anti-Christian gutter writers in the Dreyfus *affaire*?

Brazilians are extremely well informed about world affairs. The news coverage in their newspapers is ample. I know how uncomfortable the affair made me, as Consul, feel. The damage to our reputation was considerable, and eyebrows were raised in Brazil when Rufus Isaacs was subsequently made Lord Chief Justice.

Early in 1913 Lord Lonsdale wrote telling me that Mrs Lowther, wife of his cousin the Speaker (later Viscount Ullswater), was coming to Brazil for a short visit with her daughter. In order that they should see something of the interior of Brazil I arranged with the chief engineer of the Leopoldina Railway (then British) that we should take them in an observation coach to a farm belonging to Senhor Teixeira Soares, a local director of the railway. He was an influential man, so that the railway actually passed through his estate. Sometimes I would join my engineer friend, Gwyther, on the front platform of the coach. When we approached villages Gwyther pulled vigorously and continuously on a rope that set an enormous bell clanging over our heads, and the engine driver behind us set his whistle a-shrieking.

"Must there be all that noise?" I asked Gwyther.

"It's to stop anybody stretching an arm or a leg across the track," he said.

"But why on earth should anybody want to do that?" I exclaimed.

"To get compensation. To claim that the driver of the train gave no warning that the train was coming. If they can obtain damages, or a pension, they need never work again. We have had one or two such cases. So we take no chances."

At midday we arrived at Teixeira Soares's farm. The owner, a man of about 65, received us with great ceremony and had invited several local big-wigs to meet so distinguished a guest as the wife of the Speaker of the House of Commons. The dining-room was large, as all such up-country rooms are. As we sat down at a large round table for lunch, I glanced out and saw ten men in some kind of uniform lining up in the dusty sun-lit courtyard. It was a brass band. "There will be music," I whispered to Mrs Lowther. It started with a tune which, after the first few bars ,one recognized was meant to be *God Save the King*. So we all stood up while the soup got cold. Presently came another tune. "This is meant for the Brazilian national anthem," I whispered to Mrs Lowther again. "I think we should stand up." So we did. No national anthem with which I am acquainted is longer or more complicated than the Brazilian. However, eventually we did manage to get down to the business of eating and drinking. But after only ten minutes came the tune of *God Save the King* once more. Our host insisted on our remaining seated when this was followed by the Brazilian national anthem again. He explained that the band, composed of farm workers, had spent several days and nights learning how to play *God Save the King* in Mrs Lowther's honour.

Mrs Lowther, when I saw her off on her return to England, said I must come and see her, whenever I was in London, at Speaker's House. "There", she said, "you will meet all kinds of people who can be of great use to you in your career." But that never happened. The war came: the war that was "to end all wars."

Early in 1925 when I was in London on official business Leon Benvenisti, a financier who was interested in a projected British steel project in Brazil, took me to lunch at Simpson's. He introduced me to a man who sat at a table near us and who, I thought, looked very ill. It was Godfrey Isaacs, managing director of Marconi's Wireless Telegraph Co. As a much-travelled man, Isaacs was interested to hear recent news of South America. He would not join us at our table because, he said, he was on a diet.

"Did you know that my brother, Lord Reading, has been to Brazil?" he asked me.

"We have heard in Brazil", I told him, "that he ran away to sea when he was 13 or 14, and that his ship—a sailing vessel—did put in to Rio de Janeiro."

"That's right," said Godfrey Isaacs. "He used to tell us he

had gone on shore and wandered in a street near the beach; the name of it begins with S."

"Rua da Saúde," I said. "It looks on to the roads where the sailing vessels used to anchor."

Saúde means health, but I never heard a satisfactory explanation of why the street in Rio was so called. Every centuries-old city usually has some picturesque names. London has many of historical interest, but for amusing names I think Paris bears the palm: Mauvais Garçons, Quinze Vingts, Pot de Fer, and even Satan, which appropriately enough is an *impasse*.

Rio de Janeiro can emulate Paris. It has a Generosity Alley, a Regeneration Lane, and a Fraternity Avenue, as well as streets to virtues like Hope and Charity. Paris has one to Truth. Rio de Janeiro has Liberty, Perseverance, Tranquillity, New Jerusalem, and even Crocodile streets. The Anglican Church in Rio was erected in Mother-of-the-Bishop Square, the bishop himself rejoicing in the name of Joseph James Justinian de Mascarenhas Castello Branco.

One peculiarity that must strike the observant tourist in Rio de Janeiro is the quantity of streets having not names, but dates. Paris has a few, but cannot compare with Rio. There is, in fact, not a single month of the year in which several dates are not singled out for commemoration in the streets of Rio. Over thirty streets have date labels, and I am perfectly sure that not more than a handful of the inhabitants know what they are intended to commemorate.

More than twenty-four streets in Rio are named after sergeants. The reason is that many revolts and minor revolutions have been plotted in the Sergeants' Mess, and if they have been successful, grateful Newcomers in Authority have perpetuated the leading sergeant's name in a street. It must be remembered, too, that by tradition—military, if not national— the Brazilian Army, in the person of its colonels and general officers, considers itself the guardian of the nation, custodian of the republican principle, and watch-dog over every mere civilian administration of the body politic. As such, it regards it as a patriotic right and a sacred duty to intervene in matters and at moments which, it thinks, call for action on its part. The young ones pipe what their elders sing, runs a German saying; and so the Sergeants' Mess is nearly as redoubtable as the Military Club of high-ranking officers is to any civilian politicians who may happen to be at the head of the administration in the Brazilian Republic.

It is, of course, not merely sergeants who are commemorated in street names in Rio de Janeiro. No fewer than 30 field marshals, 70 generals, 32 colonels, 17 majors, 31 captains, and 34 lieutenants are thus celebrated. The Navy has sponsored only one major revolt in Brazil's history, so that in Rio street names there are only 30 admirals and 27 captains. I must in all fairness add, however, that some of these heroes of the Armed Forces are men who fought in the Paraguayan War and the two World Wars.

Monarchical titles, too, still flourish in Republican Brazil. Rio de Janeiro has street names of 17 marquesses, 16 counts, 38 viscounts, and 43 barons, while the Church is represented by two cardinals and 18 padres. There are streets without number honouring with their names doctors of every conceivable faculty. Nor have the ladies been forgotten. They must, however, be looked for, in any street index, not under their individual names, but under the letter D standing for *Dona* (Mrs). Of professors there are 54 and of lady-professors 8, while saints abound—at least, in street names.

Chapter VIII

*Interlude at the FO — Aspects of life in Rio — Critical audiences —
The National Guard — Nannies — Marriages — Pretty Boys —
What's in a Name? — Computer and Tagger.*

A FORTNIGHT before my leave (1912) was coming to an end
I received a letter from Lord Dufferin saying that "when
that sad moment" came I was to put in a short spell at
the Foreign Office before returning to Rio.

Lord Dufferin was Head of the Consular Department. His
eldest brother had been killed in the Boer War, and he had
succeeded his father in 1902. I spent a month working with
him on a scheme for rationalizing the system of Consular transfers and promotions. "Some of the transfers in recent years",
he told me, "have been, or at any rate have seemed, so
haphazard that a legend has grown up in the Office. At the
bottom of our stairs, runs the legend, is a large board listing
consuls' names. At the side is a movable kind of In and Out
indicator, or rather several of them, bearing the names of
consular posts. When any of us arrive and feel so inclined we
shift the In and Out indicators alongside some consul's name,
and that is the post he will be transferred to."

"Does the legend account for so many entries of a Consul's
statement of Services in the Foreign List having phrases like
'Transferred to Tahiti (did not proceed)' followed three
months later by 'Transferred to Timbuctoo (did not proceed)'?"
I asked.

"Ah well," said Dufferin, "the 'did not proceed' business
sometimes due to personal reasons—health or family; or
sometimes to. . . " he hesitated. . . "to a minute from the Private
Secretary or indeed from the Secretary of State."

"Does that mean influence?" I asked.

"I suppose that is the plain English of it," said Lor
Dufferin.

"I don't think I should ever refuse a transfer," I said. '
should be afraid of getting a black mark here."

"Oh, it wouldn't be black in any case," said Dufferin gail
"You will have noticed that I always use violet ink!"

"I believe, sir, that my immediate predecessor at R
actually refused a transfer to Bahia, though that would hav
meant promotion."

"Don't call me sir," said Dufferin. "It makes me feel so old
Then he went on: "Yes, Bosanquet wants no post outsic
Russia. He has passed all his career there except the sho
spell at Rio. That means limiting his chances of promotio:
But he is a good man for us to have in Russia."

Lord Dufferin was then a man of about forty-five years
age. He was short, with prematurely white hair and an enga,
ing smile. He took a really personal interest in every memb
of the Consular Service, which at that time was distinct fro
the Diplomatic Service. He asked me how I had spent n
leave. I told him, and mentioned my stay at Lowther Cast
This, I confessed, had cost me a lot in the way of tips; the
were so many people, indoor and outdoor servants, wl
seemed to expect them.

"Don't I know!" exclaimed Lord Dufferin. "I have giv
up accepting any shooting invitations simply because I cann
afford the tips they entail."

"I imagine", I said diffidently, "the Whitaker Wrig
business must have been a terrible financial blow to you ai
all your family."

"Indeed it was," he said. "And it was worse than it ne
have been."

"I think everybody knows", I said, "that though yo
father was chairman of the Globe concern, it was a pure
decorative position, and that Whitaker Wright, as managi
director, was responsible for what happened."

"No doubt," replied Lord Dufferin. "But my father felt
had a moral responsibility, and he felt it so strongly that
put everything he had into the hands of the Official Receiver

"A mere drop in the ocean," I remarked, "and really uixotic."

"Exactly," said Lord Dufferin. "And it left us all with othing. Do you know," he went on very earnestly, "during s last years my father had nothing to live on but the income om his books."

I told my friend John Gordon about this conversation when got back to Rio de Janeiro.

"Yes, it was all very sad," he commented. "It is one more stance of the stupidity of having aristocratic names figuring company prospectuses. Men like that don't know the first ing about business. They let themselves be flattered by mpany promoters. Some of them are, I suppose, glad to cket a director's fee. Apparently the British investor is tracted and even flattered by seeing prominent men on the oard of a company in which they have invested money -men with a title, or else half the alphabet after their names. ore fools they!" Gordon paused. Then he went on: "But ord Dufferin's case was a particularly sad one. He was a man ' great culture and high ideals. And look at the posts he had ld—the highest that any Englishman could aspire to: overnor-General of Canada, Viceroy of India, and Ambassa- or at Paris. As you know, I spend most of my time in Brazil; it when I am in England I dutifully go the Society rounds ith my wife. I have been to some of these do's, after the lobe crash, and seen Lady Dufferin sitting neglected in a rner of the room. Think of it! A lady who had queened it three continents!"

I used the occasion to ask Gordon something that had trigued me for some time.

"Some people in the British community here in Rio say ey are sure you are a naturalized British subject, because your ife is English, you have a home in London, and you rarely to the United States. Is that so?"

"They say that, do they?" said Gordon, quite good- mperedly. "I know something else they say. That I am a sappointed man because my wife spends all my money. How nny people are! No, I am an American citizen. I have an

office in New York, and I have never lost my rights or,
far as I know, failed in my duties as an American citizen

When I returned to Rio from my leave, I found one thir
at least settled in this unsettled world. Brazilians had made u
their minds that they would spell the name of their countr
with an S instead of a Z—Brasil. This decision had been reache
after much discussion between the High Heelers and the Lo
Heelers in the Brazilian Academy of Letters.

Early in 1913 Captain Scott's South Pole ship *Terra No.*
put in to Rio bay on her way home and, as I have relate
elsewhere,* I was able to be of some service to her commande
Lieutenant Harry Pennell, and his companions. He showe
me a little paper-back volume entitled *What a Life* which son
one, he could not remember who, had given them before the
sailed from England, saying it might help to while away son
weary hours of monotony during their stay in the Antarcti
"It certainly did that," said Pennell, "and we got no end
amusement out of it." Pennell insisted on my keeping the boo
as well as some other things, as a memento of their short sta
in Rio de Janeiro.

The book, by E. V. Lucas and George Morrow, publishe
in 1911, is made up of illustrations from a Whiteley's trac
catalogue. Around them, cut out and pasted in at the whi
of the compilers, Lucas and Morrow wove a truly touchi
story. They described it as "An Autobiography illustrated I
Whiteley's" and in a preface say: "One man searching th
pages of Whiteley's General Catalogue will find only fac
and prices; another will find what we think we have found
a deeply moving human drama." I believe the whole extrav
ganza was compiled by Lucas and Morrow when they ha
pened to be spending a rainy holiday at some English seasi
resort.

Jehu, Chilly, and Chinaman were, Pennell told me, th
names given to ponies on the Scott expedition. I do n
remember the names of the huskies who panted on the de
of the *Terra Nova* on their way home in the heat of Rio

---

*In *British Consul.*

Janeiro. Pennell, whom I met again later in Albania, was killed in the First World War.

Writing in 1938, Gondin da Fonseca, a witty Brazilian journalist, spoke of the slab architecture which, he said, had destroyed the individuality of Rio de Janeiro, and he deplored the passing of the city's "Bohemia of bygone days." The Bohemia to which he alludes was still flourishing when I first went to Brazil. But during the First World War its lustre was dimmed and by the end of the war it had almost entirely disappeared. By then the North Americans had 'discovered' Brazil, and under the formidable pressure of Our Way of Life the Bohemia of Rio de Janeiro and much else that was typically Brazilian was crushed out of existence.

The first café-concert to open in Rio de Janeiro was named *Paradise*; that was in 1857. But the Bohemia of which Gondin da Fonseca was thinking was rather the literary world that met in bookshops like Garnier, in the entrances of newspaper offices, in modest cafés, or in the shady streets that admit no vehicles, like the rua do Ouvidor or the rua Gonçalves Dias— the former named after the designation of the Judge appointed to *hear* complaints, the latter after Brazil's greatest lyrical poet. In this street was the *Confeitaria Colombo*, which was the capital of Bohemia, but only after 5 p.m.

The confiserie was installed with considerable luxury. Its walls were faced with immense plate-glass mirrors supplied by Pilkington's, the first of the kind to be put up in Rio, just as Rio's first plate-glass shop windows were fitted for Mappin & Webb in the rua do Ouvidor. Not only cakes and confectionery, but drinks of all kinds, hard as well as soft, were served at the Colombo. Between 3.30 and 5 p.m. it was the chic thing for ladies out shopping to meet there for afternoon tea. Not coffee. Brazil being the largest coffee-producing country in the world, obviously High Society had to drink tea, just as it is to-day "the thing" to drink whisky in wine-producing countries like France and Italy.

At 4.50 p.m. an onlooker would have observed that the ladies in the *Confeitaria Colombo* began looking at their watches, paid their bills, and made a dignified exit. By 5 p.m. not one

I

of them was left. The waiters whisked the damask tea cloths off the tables, and in a few minutes the Bohemians would make their entry and sit at the marble-topped tables, closely followed by the reigning beauties, the *dames galantes*, as Brantôme calls them, and some others. Soon the place would be full of chatter, laughter, and cigarette smoke, and the fusillade of wit and witty scandal would last until 6.30, when everybody began leaving for dinner. By 7 p.m. the *Confeitaria Colombo* had closed its doors.

The owner of establishment in the years I am writing about (1910–14) was a Portuguese named França. Immaculately dressed, he ran the place like a consummate artist. He was courtesy itself and the repository of many confidences. Which he never betrayed. The Portuguese envoy at Rio from 1901 until the republican revolution of 1910–11 in that country was named Camello Lampreia. His first name means camel. Emilio de Menezes, Brazil's most famous wit—his wit was always mordant, often cruel—once observed to his companions seated round a Colombo table: "You know, with his polished manners, França ought to be representing Portugal instead of that camel Lampreia, who is more cut out to serve behind a market stall." An instance of justice suffering at the expense of wit. Lampreia, whom I knew well, was dignified and courteous, but a staunch monarchist in republican Brazil.

The *Confeitaria Colombo* was a rendezvous not only for literary men, but for politicians too. That was because so many newspaper men, writers, and politicians in those days were brothers-in-arms. They seemed to confirm Robert Louis Stevenson's opinion that human affairs are advanced not by so-called strong, silent men, but by talkers. Certainly there was much talk, some of it very good talk, between five and half-past six at the *Colombo*. There was plenty of night life, too, in Rio, though that had nothing to do with Bohemia.

When the Municipal Theatre at Rio de Janeiro was built, in 1908, it was modelled, on a much smaller scale, on Garnier's opera house in Paris. But for some reason that I never fathomed, the Prefecture decided that the ground floor, below the auditorium, should be fitted out as a restaurant, with mosaic

and marbles and bulls, to be known as *The Assyrian*. It opened
in the evenings and was used as a café and dance floor. Anything less calculated to inspire gaiety than the winged bull's
heads and stiff-bearded faces carved in cold, green marble and
presumably representing Assyrian art it would be hard to
imagine. Outside, lurid placards hinted at wild orgies. Inside,
sad-faced young men at so much an hour dragged round
elderly females to the music of melancholy tangos and mincing
ball-room *maxixes*.

A word about this Brazilian dance, which, like the *samba*,
seems to have travelled all over the world. First of all, pronounce
Mahcheechee with the accent on the second syllable. Secondly,
it is not a ball-room dance. The real *maxixe* has to be seen
danced not in the emasculated indoor version of drawing-
rooms, but in the streets and in its uninhibited form as danced
in clubs and popular dance halls in Brazil. Only Brazilians
know how to dance it. Presumably natives of Rio de Janeiro
dance it best, since it originated in that city.

The *maxixe* is a fruit of the gourd or pumpkin family, and it is
perhaps no mystery that it should have given its name to a
quick two-four dance. The *maxixe* vegetable has clinging
tendrils—and that is how Brazilians dance their dance.

Samba is one of a score of names for Brazilian rum, but as a
dance its origin is African, more especially by reason of its
syncopated time, though the town *samba* is quite different
from the country *samba*.

One form of amusement in pre-1914 days in Rio was to
watch wrestling bouts on the stage of a theatre. Straw hats
with sharply pointed rims were then worn by men. The
wrestlers were from all countries, and the style was proclaimed
to be *luta romana*, which I take to be Graeco-Roman wrestling;
but I am no expert. The audience had their favourites, and
had, no doubt, bets on the results. Those who had backed a
loser kicked up a tremendous row, swore the judge (or is he a
referee?) had been bribed, and then, using their straw hats as
disks, spun them on to the stage; walking-sticks and other
missiles followed.

After a while, Rio tired of men wrestlers and engaged women. There was the same pandemonium as with the men. But it was always a mulatto girl who was the favourite.

A South American tour including Rio de Janeiro regularly brought some of the world's best performers—Caruso, Scotti, Tito Ruffo, Tetrazzini, Barrientos, Pavlova, Nijinsky, Lucien Guity, and Yvonne Printemps, to mention but a few. The First World War upset this routine, and Rio had to make do for some years afterwards with third-rate companies. One year, Mascagni brought out a company. I went to a performance of *La Gioconda*. Mascagni conducted; the singers were really very bad, especially the tenor. I happened to have a seat in the stalls, and as the opera proceeded I could feel at first and then hear unrest in all the tiers behind. Eventually, the gallery broke out into whistles and cat-calls at the end of a particularly badly sung aria. However, the row calmed down, and the opera proceeded without further mishap. The point is that merely to have a big name in the world of music, like Mascagni, heading an *ensemble* meant nothing to the Rio audience which can be violently critical and, at times, wildly enthusiastic. It is true that the Brazilians did not found an Academy of Music until quite recently—in 1945—with Heitor Villa-Lobos as its first president; but their appreciation of music has always been keenly critical. At the head of the critics I should place João Itiberê da Cunha, a very charming personality who wrote under the pen-name JIC.

I assisted at another incident, similar to the one I have just recounted about Mascagni. This time it was not at the Municipal Theatre, but at the old Theatro Republica, where the impresario, in the lean post-war years that I have referred to, did try to atone for being able to present to the public only a third-rate Italian opera company. He reduced the prices of all the seats, so that the theatre was sold out at the first performance. The opera chosen was Ambroise Thomas's *Hamlet*. The locally recruited orchestra played indifferently well. Then Hamlet appeared and began singing. The effect was not bad; it was excruciating. He was a baritone, sadly out of tune, and the audience let him know it. He walked to the footlights, put up both his hands, the orchestra stopped playing. Then amid complete silence he addressed the audience with magnificent irony, saying: *"Questo per me? Aspetate il tenore!"* ("Was that meant for me? Wait till you hear the tenor!") There was an immense shout of laughter, and the opera was resumed. The baritone was right. The tenor was worse.

Arthur Henry Savage Landor, grandson of "the unsubduable old Roman," was the first of many modern journalist-travellers who have come to Brazil in order to make money by writing and lecturing about their Adventures in Wonderland. Like others who followed him, he talked and wrote in a minor key. It is a device calculated to exalt the writer's merits to major heights. Landor scoffed at Theodore Roosevelt's sensational books, and with some reason I think, for Roosevelt, who was accompanied by a Brazilian geological expert, Euzebio de Oliveira, whom I knew very well, never "discovered" any "River of Doubt." He discovered nothing. There was nothing to discover. It had all been done, long since, by Brazilian explorers and engineers.

Landor was, of course, an experienced traveller. To me he always used the same phrase: "I am going to walk across Brazil," and then he would add with a smile, "and I shall not dress up, like Roosevelt. I shall go just as I am dressed now". Which was in a lounge suit and a straw boater. He gave an account of his "walk" in a book published in 1913.

During the many weeks he remained in Rio de Janeiro before setting out to cross Mato Grosso, Landor made friends with a Brazilian journalist, Colonel Ernest Senna. Landor, who spoke Italian perfectly, was soon at home in Portuguese, which was the only language Senna spoke, though he was a fervent admirer of all things and most people English. When Landor introduced us I was rather surprised that the Colonel was such a puny little man; but I soon tumbled to the fact that he was a colonel in the *Guarda Nacional*. This was a kind of Home Guard first recruited by Padre Diogo Antonio Feijó— an "energetic old man," Brazilian historians call him—who was Minister of Justice under the Regency, while the little

Emperor, Dom Pedro II, was only 5 years old. That was in 1831 and there was much unrest, with clamours for abolishing the monarchy. So Padre Feijó created a Home Guard, which was never disbanded. In later years it became a convenient way of conferring honorary military rank on local *chefes políticos*—influential provincial landowners or others who could swing votes.

I never met anybody below the rank of major in the *Guarda Nacional*. Most of them were colonels—up-country big-wigs, who in talk and on the stage were stock-characters as victims of the wiles of Circe and the smooth tongue of swindlers when they came to Rio de Janeiro, the capital of Brazil. The "Colonel" in this sense is a character so well established in the Brazilian way of life that the entry in Portuguese dictionaries under Colonel runs: "Commander of a regiment; and (Brazilian usage) fellow who pays the expenses."

Ernesto Senna was a *colonel*. When I knew him he was 52 years of age, but in mien an old man. And he was poor. Perhaps because he had already "paid the expenses," or perhaps because he was an exception to the rule. He served for many years on the staff of the *Jornal do Commercio*, then the most important Rio daily, and he had the entrée everywhere. Hence his usefulness to Landor, who was negotiating for a Brazilian subsidy before setting out on his walk across the country. I ran into Senna one night at some very official function in honour of which he had dressed up in his colonel's uniform. With the best will in the world, I could hardly keep from laughing. He was a thin little man and very short. The gorgeous uniform of blue and gold fitted him badly and the sword was enormous, far too big for him to manage. It kept getting between his legs as he moved about. I had imagined till then that this sort of thing only happened to stage-land comedians.

I saw a lot of Landor. We often dined together. He struck me as a cultured man, and if one had not known his record as a traveller one would have said that he was far from robust. He was short and slightly built. His manner was almost timid, or appeared so until one engaged him in conversation. His keen brown eyes darted all round the room of the hotel where we usually dined (*Hôtel dos Estrangeiros*, now no more). He came to see me when he returned from Mato Grosso. He looked worn and much thinner. He pulled up one trouser leg to prove he had contracted beri-beri, though I had not questioned his statement at all. We dined together again; but he had nothing to say about his journey and I did not press him. The only thing of interest he told me was that the mule with all his best photographic plates had disappeared, plates and all, in a difficult river crossing.

From time to time during my official work I found that DBS had several meanings. In Board of Trade and Merchant Shipping parlance the initials stood for Distressed British Seaman. In general terms they might mean Distressed British Subject, which might include governesses in trouble. A typical case would be that a Brazilian senator or deputy, while on a mission or other official visit to Europe with his wife, had engaged and brought back with them an English governess for their children. The first I would know about it would be a visit, several weeks later, from the governess who would come to me "for advice." Her trouble? The lady of the house was making her life unbearable. The reason? Jealousy, though the governess did not use that word. Even with my bachelor experience I knew that all Brazilian women were convinced that all Brazilian husbands were philanderers, capable of a thousand infidelities. That the lady in the British governess cases should be highly respectable and incapable of encouraging, much less provoking, what the Brazilian wife suspected, or rather pretended to suspect her of—all that counted for nothing. She was the Other Woman, and was living under the same roof.

Having assured myself that the governess had no ill-treatment to complain of, merely scenes and tantrums, the solution was that the best plan would be for her to return to England. Usually the employer came to see me and paid the governess's fare home. No allusion would be made to the cause of her departure by either of us.

In this line of trouble—that is, of a domestic nature—a far

more awkward case was when a Scotch lady married to a German came to see me and complained that her husband was brutal to her. He stormed into my office one day, having suspected that she would call on me, and, as I turned him out, I was quite sure of his capacity for brutality. But I could do nothing for the lady, except advise her to consult a local lawyer. She was no longer a British subject.

To the best of my knowledge none of the twentieth century British nannies has written a book about her experiences in Brazil. One in the nineteenth century did; but hers was rather a special case because she was engaged to instruct the eldest daughter of the Emperor Dom Pedro I. Maria Graham was the wife of a captain in the Royal Navy and accompanied her husband to Brazil, where she stayed little more than a year (1821-23). It is obvious from what she tells us that she was a considerable snob. She is best known, however, not from the diary of her stay in Brazil, but for her *Little Arthur's History of England*, of which seventy editions appear to have been published.

I knew an English governess who was employed in the Matarazzo family. Francesco Matarazzo, who had come to Brazil from Italy as a poor immigrant in the 1870's, was then the richest industrialist in Brazil. He was a master of the merger magic, as the title of his enterprises still shows: Indústrias Reunidas Francesco Matarazzo. He was a real character, studious of the welfare of his employees. He lived for his business, and when he came home tired and his wife (whom he adored) began an interminable recountal of all the happenings of their large family, including many in-laws, he would put cotton wool in his ears and go to sleep. They lived in a magnificent palace in São Paulo. But the old man was of austere habit himself. His eldest son and daughter-in-law had an English governess for their children. Like all Italians, the old man was very fond of children. But I have heard him complain to his grandchildren in Italian, with a wry smile: "I can't talk to you little ones any more. You only talk English."

Of Consular marriages, I performed over twenty while I was Acting Consul General. It was often hard to convince the couple on two points: first, that the Solemnization of Marriage in the Anglican Church, however desirable, would be no legal proof of regular marriage in Brazil or even in Great Britain, and that it was the Consular marriage, or a *lex loci* marriage at which the Consul assisted, which alone would be registered at Somerset House. The other point both the padre Graham and I insisted on was that if the parties were residing in Brazil, a marriage by Brazilian law was advisable, as well as the marriages in the Church and the Consulate. There were, in effect, three marriage ceremonies where one of the parties was British.

As in many other countries, it is quite easy to get married in Brazil. It is not so easy to get a divorce; indeed, in theory it is impossible, though there are ways of getting a marriage annulled, if you know how.

One day at the Consulate-General two good-looking young Brazilians, immaculately dressed, insisted on seeing me personally and were introduced. This was in 1910, a few months after my arrival. With an air of great mystery one of them spread before me a beautifully bound album, containing official rubber stampings of two Brazilian ministries over sprawling signatures, besides a number of other signatures. It was explained to me that a collection was being made for a charity dear to the heart of a Brazilian Minister. But it was to be a surprise for him. Hence the secrecy. Leading public men were subscribing, and, as I could see, two of my Consular colleagues had already subscribed. The Diplomatic Corps would be approached later. I saw that one of the Consuls had given 100 milréis, the equivalent then of about £6. So I gave an equal amount. Full of thanks and bows the young men departed. I told pro-Consul Pullen, our shipping clerk, a man of about sixty and formerly a prosperous British merchant, what had been the mission of the mysterious young men. "Sounds fishy," was his comment. About ten days later I showed him a paragraph from the *Jornal do Commercio*. "You were right," I said. "It was fishy."

The young men must have made quite a good thing out of

their collecting mission before they slipped up through over-confidence and were arrested. A high official whom they hoped to dupe saw that one of the two imposing signatures that had impressed me was a blatant forgery. How they got hold of the two ministerial rubber stamps was not explained. The young men were well connected, and nothing more was heard of the incident.

The newspaper account of their misdoings was headed *Moços Bonitos*—Pretty Boys. It was one of a number of names by which gilded young misdoers have been known in Brazil. Others that I recall are: Rascals, Dainty Ones, Insinuators, Softies, Dandies, and Super-Elegants.

One of the most interesting men I met in those early years of my official life in Brazil was David Hannay, the author of many books on ships and sailors. He wrote for a number of London evening papers—there were many more than two then!—and from Brazil was writing some articles for *The Times*. We had lunch at the City Club and afterwards, in the quiet of the little lounge when we were alone, we talked of books, among them *Trilby*. I said I thought George du Maurier must have been extremely gratified at its resounding success as a novel and, later, as a play when Beerbohm Tree produced it.

"No doubt he was pleased," said Hannay; "but he could never really enjoy its success."

"Why not?" I asked.

"It came too late in his life," replied Hannay. "He died two years after it was published, and his health was not good." And then he added, wistfully, I thought: "You have to be young to really enjoy success."

Except for very occasional visits from people like Hannay, British newspapers had no direct or permanent contacts in Brazil in the early years of this century. However, British financiers and shareholders in the many British public utility companies in Brazil, as well as holders of Brazilian Government bonds, were kept in touch with Brazilian developments by a weekly publication, *Wileman's Review*. This publication was owned and edited by an Englishman, J. P. Wileman.

This Englishman's position at that time was unique. It dated from the 1890's. The President of the Republic from 1898 to 1902 was Campos Salles, whose Minister of Finance was Joaquim Murtinho. These two men thoroughly reformed Brazilian finances, which had lapsed into disarray during the turbulent years that followed the inauguration of the republican régime. They employed no magic formula. They merely introduced the practice of honest administration, avoiding extravagance in public spending, and, most important of all, setting a personal example of thrift. Campos Salles used to ride from his residence to the presidential palace on a bicycle.

One of the things that required overhauling, however, was the out-moded system of book-keeping of the public accounts; or, more exactly, the real need was for an up-to-date system of departmental statistics, on which a Finance Minister could base his budgets. To help him in this work Joaquim Murtinho picked on a Briton, J. P. Wileman, a mining engineer who had knocked about South America without ever "striking it rich," but who had the reputation of being skilled at figures and was an educated man.

Wileman founded and was appointed director of a Brazilian Commercial Statistics Department, and trained a few young Brazilian enthusiasts to run it. One of them, Léo d'Affonseca, was head of the department during much of my time in Brazil. I found him a helpful and competent official.

When the Campos Salles/Joaquim Murtinho administration ended, the Government coffers were full, and the next President, Rodrigues Alves (1902-06), used the greater part of the funds he had inherited to transform the capital, Rio de Janeiro, from an old, dilapidated colonial town into a modern city.

More loans had been raised in London (Brazilian authorities never had the loan of a single American dollar until 1921) and it was *Wileman's Review* which kept The City posted week by week on what was going on in Brazil, more especially anything of interest to the sixty and more British joint stock companies then operating in Brazil.

When I knew him Wileman had resigned from his job in the Statistical Department, but he had the entrée into most Ministers, though not into all at all times, for Wileman was an irascible creature and, like so many of that type, easily took offence. He had, quite rightly, a high appreciation of his own abilities, but would brook no contradiction or even disagreement on any particular bee he might have in his bonnet at any given moment. I knew him well and sometimes dined at his house with him and his three daughters and one or two guests. But these little dinner parties were a trial. He would insist on talking shop. Finance and trade were his only topics of conversation, though that is the wrong word. It was a monologue.

"You agree with me, don't you?" he would say after three minutes' non-stop speaking.

"There is much in what you say," one would rejoin; "but I think one has to remember . . ."

"No really," he would break in. "The case is quite simple, because, as I was saying. . . ."

For several decades now, Brazilian printing works have turned out copy in various languages. In the early years of the century, however, it was not easy to get anything printed in English. It was particularly difficult in the case of a review. Accordingly Wileman set up a printing press of his own—The English Printing Works—which, besides printing his *Review*, did other work in Portuguese. For his printing in English he engaged a linotype compositor from England. Indeed, that was my first introduction to Wileman. His compositor came to the Consulate to complain to me that he could stand Wileman's tantrums no longer and wanted me to pay his passage home. I called on Wileman to hear his side of the story. It was that the compositor was a grumbler and not much good at his job. The matter was patched up by the compositor agreeing to remain until another man could be engaged in London to replace him. A couple of years later, the same story of compositor versus Wileman was repeated, and shortly afterwards yet again. This time, the new arrival called on me and told me that Wileman was on the Black

List at home, not as a bad payer, but as an employer whose temper made it impossible for anybody to work with him. I am afraid Wileman was, in fact, a bully; and to his grown-up son too.

His articles were never without interest, and sometimes very good. His main support came from the advertisements placed in his *Review* by British joint stock concerns operating from London in Brazil. Wileman was very fond of using Latin tags to point a moral rather than adorn a tale. The articles were prosy, but one watched out for the end tag. It rarely failed to appear. *Ab uno disce omnes* would close a paragraph on a mismanaged concern, while the punctual payment of interest owing would evoke a final *O si sic omnes*. A long article urging some reform on the Federal Government would close with *Hoc opus, hic labor est*, and *O fortunatos nimium* would end a paragraph telling Brazilian coffee planters that they did not know when they were well off.

There had been other weekly publications in English before Wileman founded his review in 1908, the most notable being the *Anglo-Brazilian Times*, owned and edited by a Briton in the confidence of the Emperor, William Scully. There were others, too, after the First World War, but they did not handle economic matters; their purpose was to record the social doings of the British community. Some prospered; others did not; but eventually all were condemned to extinction. In the supra-nationalist 1960's it was decreed, one day, that no foreign-language newspaper should be published in Brazil. Supra-nationalist in this context, and in some others elsewhere, does not mean internationalist, but ultranationalist. If some publications in the English language are to be found today in Brazil, the How and Why of their appearance is too complicated a story for me to touch on. What I can affirm with absolute assurance is that the days of Scully and Wileman are "lost and gone for ever."

Chapter IX

Dalmatia — Albania — Croats and Serbs — Venice — Milan —
Berne — Bâle — Dyes and TNT — The FO and a watch —
Spies and Cushies — Temple of Peace — Neutrality discerning.

IN JANUARY, 1914, I was posted to Ragusa. This was the
first time I held a Royal Commission signed by the King,
and I was very proud of it. My jurisdiction was the Austrian
province of Dalmatia. The change was abrupt from the busy
port of Rio de Janeiro, with hundreds of British ships putting
in every year, and from a thriving commercial centre with a
large British community. The intention was, Lord Dufferin
told me when I called at the Foreign Office, that after the
burden and heat of the busiest post in Brazil I should have a
more restful post, though it was one from which I should be
able to keep an eye on Balkan and other Near Eastern political
developments; and there would be naval movements to be
watched too. That was my official assignment. Things turned
out rather differently for most of us in 1914, I mean from what
we expected.

In June, 1914, after a few days' leave in England, I was given
some despatches to take to our High Commissioner at Durazzo,
Sir Harry Lamb. While I was with him Admiral Sir Ernest
Troubridge came in. He was a bluff, cheery sailor, with a Lloyd
George shock of white hair. He was the personification of
optimism, and this surprised me, for he had a most difficult
and invidious task to perform. It was, by a display of naval
power, to persuade the Albanians to behave. Troubridge's
own squadron consisted of the *Defence* (flag), the *Black Prince*,
the *Duke of Edinburgh*, and the *Warrior*. There was an Austrian
admiral with a couple of ships, and there were Italian, French,
and, last but far, far from least, two German ships, *Goeben*

and *Breslau*. The Albanians were singularly unimpressed by this show of naval might. They disliked and mistrusted the arrangements the Great Powers had made for their welfare by appointing an ex-Prussian Guardsman to rule over them with the title of Mpret. On shore, there were a few Dutch gendarmes, too, similarly sent by the Great Powers to protect the Mpret. This gentleman, Prince von Wied, with a British artillery officer as his private secretary, never ventured outside his palace. The whole affair had many of the elements of a comic opera, for beyond the immediate precincts of the Palace the rest of Albania was perfectly happy misgoverning itself. The dénouement is part of the history of the First World War.

That Albania should ever have become enamoured of Chinese communism would seem quite impossible, if it had not happened. But in this context Albania does not necessarily mean Albanians. When I was there I went to Valona with Miss Edith Durham, whose knowledge of the country and the people was unique. Her books on the Balkans can be studied with profit today. She quite naturally had no patience with the imposition of a foreign ruler on the country, and would, I am sure, from my long conversations with her on the spot and twenty-five years later in London, have made a very clear distinction between the present-day rulers of the country and its people. As a nation, Albania is the odd-man-out among Balkan peoples.

Before and during the First World War Albania was coveted by Italy; but no conquerors, whether Goths or Romans, Normans or Serbs or Turks, ever succeeded in subduing the Albanians, much less absorbing or amalgamating them. It would be no exaggeration, I think, to say that every Albanian is a Scanderbeg, and the probable explanation of Albania's present-day pro-Chinese attitudes is due not to any love of China or things Chinese, but to fear of domination by Slavs, who are her neighbours. Serbs and Russians may quarrel among themselves; but in Albanian eyes they are both Slavs, and historically Serb domination was Slav domination. When the time is ripe, Albania will abandon her China policy as easily as Scanderbeg deserted Turkey, renounced Islam, defeated a Turkish army that outnumbered him ten to one, and maintained Albanian independence until his death more than twenty years later.

In Ragusa—I find it hard to call it Dubrovnik—I noticed that the local Croatian men of substance, though dressed in national costume, invariably carried a black Western umbrella, which, incidentally, did not go at all well with their gay-coloured clothes. They would congregate and chat near the Rector's Palace, but when they walked along the Stradone in the glaring sunshine they would open their umbrellas. The summer sun reverberating from the stone-flagged main street, the Stradone, was fierce, and a downward pointed open umbrella gave ample protection for face and shoulders.

The beautiful Dalmatian coast seems less beautiful to me by the change from the pleasant-sounding Italian names to their Slav equivalents: Spalato to Split (which sounds like *le grand écart* in a French music hall), Pola to Pulj, Gravosa to Gruz, and so on. On the other hand the Bocche di Cattaro could not cease to be impressive even under the name of Kotor. But does one obliterate history or wreck reputations by changing names?

Dalmatia in the pre-1914 days was a Kingdom and Crown Land administered by a Governor at Zara, Ragusa being one of thirteen "district captaincies" into which the Crown Land was divided. The war came upon us before arrangements were completed for my official call on the Governor; but my relations with Dr Renkin, the District Captain, were soon established and cordial. I was in Paris, on my way back to Ragusa from a fortnight in England, when the Austrian Archduke Francis-Ferdinand and his wife were assassinated at Serajevo. I spent some time with Reginald Ray, who had been Legation translator in Petropolis and was working in Paris. He pooh-poohed my view that the Serajevo affair meant European war; so did other people I met in Paris.

When I called on Renkin at Ragusa to announce my return and to express my regrets at the assassination, he told me how gratified he had been at the genuine grief manifested by the local Croatian notables who had called on him to condole. He told me his satisfaction was the greater because he had not expected them to do this.

"But why not?" I said. "Surely it was only natural that they should deplore what happened at Serajevo."

"From the humanitarian point of view no doubt that is so," said the District Captain. "But you must remember that however benign our administration—and I think you will agree that it is not harsh—we Austrians are regarded by them as oppressors, traditionally so regarded. The tradition is that they should hate us, so that as the Austrian heir apparent has been murdered, one would expect them to be elated. It is true that it is the Serbs who have committed this dastardly crime, not the Croats; and Serbs and Croats do not love each other. Still, I was gratified to find that the Croatian notables here seemed genuinely sorry."

"It was certainly an atrocious business," I observed to Renkin as I came away; "and one cannot make heroes of murderers."

As we now know, however, that is precisely what the Serbs have done. Even the footprints of the assassin, where he stood to do the deed, have been preserved—in cement!

In the matter of hatred, Renkin was right. Croats and Serbs, however much they may dislike each other, both hated the Austrians. I had an instance of this a few days before we declared war on Austria in 1914. I went to the local bank, an Austrian institution, and told the manager that I foresaw an imminent rupture between my country and Austria. Whether I managed to get out of Ragusa or not, I should want money, and I asked him to cash a cheque on London for £50—in gold, if possible. He left his room and presently came back with a scoop of gold coins. "All we have in gold at the moment," he said, "is the equivalent of £35 in sovereigns and francs. Make me out a cheque for that amount. Of course, I shouldn't be doing this. But we are not at war yet, and I am glad to help you, for you represent a country that will be defending freedom. I manage an Austrian bank. But I am a Croat, and I hate the Austrians."

K

"What has happened to our friend Cingrija?" I asked. He was the Mayor of Ragusa. "He came to me the other day and said he was going to South America, and I gave him some letters of introduction to people there."

"There you are," said the bank manager. "What *has* happened to him? Where is he? He went north to Trieste. I feel sure they have arrested him, probably at Zara."

"But on what grounds?" I asked.

"Merely because he is a Croat patriot. And," he went on with a smile, "if you don't go now, I shall be under suspicion for having talked so long with the British Consul."

I had found in Albania that Greeks and Albanians were at daggers drawn over a strip of land known as the Epirus, and I remembered that in Belgrade I had learnt how Macedonia was a bone of contention between Serbs, Greeks, and Bulgarians. No doubt Dr Renkin, the District Captain, was right when he spoke to me at Ragusa about "traditional hatreds"—and not only in the Balkans, I am afraid.

"If you want to get to know Venice really well, you must walk, and forget there are such things as gondolas." That was what Dr Willis had told me when I was dining with him one day at his residence in the Rio de Janeiro Botanical Gardens. In the pre-1914 days he had come from Ceylon to take charge of the Rio Gardens. He was a man of wide knowledge and it was interesting to listen to him talking about Oriental beliefs and superstitions.

I found Venice a great relief from the anxious days I had spent in Ragusa wondering how I was to get out of Austria after our declaration of war. Italy was neutral. Hundreds of British tourists in Venice clamoured that we—Gerald Campbell, the Consul there, and I—should stop the war in order that they might travel back to Great Britain across France not only in security, but in comfort too. Mobilization, military service, disruption of civilian life, fear of enemy invasion— these and other war conditions had absolutely no meaning for them. I think what hit them most was that no bank and no hotel would take their English money. As a matter of history, the Foreign Office acted with commendable dispatch, and a liner, the *Cretic*, was sent to Genoa to pick up all British tourists in that part of the world and bring them home. Even so, I had to calm down an angry deputation who wanted to know what precautions had been taken to protect them against enemy submarines!

Much of my time in Venice was spent in gleaning and sending home news from across the Austrian frontier. Arthur Moore of *The Times* turned up from Albania; so did Miss Durham. There were British refugees from Trieste as well.

In November 1914, I was posted to Bâle. Perhaps its German name Basel is more appropriate, for there was nothing French about it any more, except—and the exception is a big one— the French Consul-General there, Louis Farges. He had been Chef du Protocole at the Quai d'Orsay, and had met and admired Sir Charles Dilke. He was not an admirer of President Wilson. Farges was the personification of all that is best in the French way of life: he was a man of wide culture and wise counsels, witty and perspicacious, frank and friendly.

One-third of the population at Bâle was German-born and one-third German inclined; but the rest were staunchly Swiss and doggedly independent. Swiss dialects are as numerous as the so-called German-Swiss cantons, and as their school text books were all in High German, it was not unnatural that in adult life they should look at things from the German angle. I knew enough of Germany and Switzerland to feel at home in Bâle.

I stopped off at Milan on my way to Switzerland from Venice, and had long chats with John Towsey, the Consul, and his honorary Vice-Consul Rose who had formerly been a prosperous merchant. Both men had spent many years in Milan, and from what they told me and what I heard outside, it was clear that the Germans in north Italy felt on top of the world. In any case, the moneyed classes in Italy were inclined to be pro-German; the people pro-Allies; as was the case in Spain.

My next stop was at Berne, to report to our Minister, Evelyn Grant Duff. He and his wife were kindness itself. He was always calm and unruffled in appearance; but he could, when the occasion demanded it, be very firm in his dealings with the Swiss authorities. The normal staff of the Legation consisted of a First Secretary and an Attaché. The Secretary was Ellice Michael Hicks Beach, a man of about forty. He told me that in fourteen years in the Diplomatic Service he had served in no fewer than seven countries. I told him I was on my way to beating that record, for in a single year (1914) I should have held posts in four different countries. I doubt if the Diplomatic Service held many attractions for Hicks Beach. Perhaps he shared rather in the financial wizardry attributed to his cousin, the former Conservative Chancellor of the Exchequer.

To handle the many complicated problems created by the war, the staff at the Legation was considerably augmented. Lord Acton, for instance, came to Berne after having had to leave his post as Minister at Darmstadt. He was the man I had met some years before when he came to Zurich, the son of the historian who had sat at the feet of Cardinal Wiseman and, later, of Dr Döllinger in Munich. While he was at Berne Acton was awarded the KCVO. I happened to be sitting opposite him at a desk in the Chancery when news of the award reached him in a FO despatch.

"I see I have been awarded the KCVO," he told us, adding with some emphasis, "but this has nothing to do with my diplomatic job. It's because I happen to be a Lord-in-Waiting."

The point was a nice one for those to whom decorations mean something, for Acton's chief, the Minister, Grant Duff, was only Commander—of another order: a CMG.

Another refugee from Germany at the Berne Legation was Frank Savery, who had been employed in our Legation at Munich for a few years without being on the "establishment". He was a scholarly, fair-complexioned man of thirty-two with flaming red hair and moustache. His large green eyes seemed to stare quizzingly on the world, but he was a gay companion, soft-spoken, and a most entertaining conversationalist. When war was declared in that fateful holiday month of August,

1914, our Minister at Munich was away, so it fell to Savery to burn cyphers and papers. We compared notes, for I had nearly set my flat on fire when engaged on a similar task in Ragusa. My neighbour, a Montenegrin lady, feared I would set the whole house alight. In Savery's case, angry Bavarians thought he was trying to burn down their capital!

My job at Bâle sometimes took me to Berne. When it did, I made a point of spending some hours with Savery. His witty comments on European events, and not least on the cosmopolitan crowd at Berne were always refreshing. His knowledge on things that he thought important made him exacting, sometimes to the point of pedantry. One day when we were having a drink at the Bellevue bar he told me he had had a most tiring time with some Americans that morning. At that time many American do-gooders followed in Colonel House's wake, and there were quite a number of rich Americans whose permanent residence was in Switzerland. An American lady had consulted Savery on a question of protocol. She could not have gone to a better authority. At a dinner party she was giving she proposed to seat an Italian prince on her right and an Austrian archduke on her left. Savery told her she would have to reverse those places.

"But one's a prince, and the other's only a dook," protested the lady.

"An archduke," corrected Savery.

"But the other's a *prince*!" urged the lady.

"Princes in Italy are five a penny," said Savery, "and in any case an Austrian archduke would take precedence over most princes in any country."

Savery was genuinely grieved that a well-educated American lady should require so much convincing—if she was really convinced!—about such hierarchical distinctions.

Incidentally, I never met a Swiss who expressed any sort of pride in the knowledge that the whole race of Habsburg archdukes and emperors stem from Switzerland. Several of the Bâle families I knew could claim origins even more ancient.

One of Bâle's aristocratic ladies, who had lived for some time in the United States, told me she thought Boston was the most snobbish town on earth. "I expect they have told you that Bâle is," she added gaily.

"Oh, one hears all sorts of things at the *Casino*, where I usually dine," I said. "And one never believes all one hears, especially in war time. In any case, I find everybody here very friendly. Officially, there are some trials. Your Chief of Police, Dr Blocher, for instance. He persists in impounding all British passports as though we were enemies of your country."

"But he is a red, red Socialist," exclaimed my hostess, genuinely troubled. "And you mustn't judge us Bâlois by him."

"I don't," I assured her. "In fact he rather amused me when I arrived and paid him the usual official courtesy call. Without the slightest provocation on my part he read me a lecture on the superiority of German *Kultur*, the untrustworthiness of the French, and the wrong-headedness of the British."

This brought shocked disclaimers from all the Swiss at the dinner table. But I assured them I had lived long enough in Zurich as a young man to know precisely how much and how little to attach to what the Bâle Chief of Police had told me about Swiss sentiment.

It was understandable that business men in Switzerland should dislike having their normal trade with Germany curtailed, and in some cases completely stopped, owing to the British blockade policy. One of my jobs was to see that goods sent to Great Britain from Bâle were genuinely Swiss. My other commercial task was in many respects even more important. It was to see that the raw materials for dyes, which apparently contain a large dose of potential TNT, did not find their way from Great Britain to Germany, but solely to the Swiss dye industries for which they were intended. All this meant keeping a tight control over shipping and forwarding arrangements, once I had organized them, and coming to working arrangements with the Bâle dye works, of which there were four.

After fifteen months at Bâle I was posted back to Brazil, this time as Commercial Attaché to our Legation. One day I received a surprise visit from a deputation of the directorates of the dye works, and was ceremoniously handed a letter, dated January 28, 1916, as follows:—

"The news of your impending departure from this town has been received by the four undersigned firms with real sorrow and regret. While heartily congratulating you on your promotion to an important post abroad, we all feel we are losing a friend, who during his too short term of office here has at all times been anxious to entertain most pleasant relations with the representatives of the industrial and commercial interests of Bâle.

"In these critical times when almost unsurmountable difficulties have to be faced, your wise and judicious support has been of the highest value and importance to us. We therefore cannot let this opportunity pass without expressing our sincerest thanks for all you have done to facilitate our relations with your great country, and assuring you we shall never forget the efficient help you have lent us at the present juncture.

"May we ask you to accept the accompanying souvenir of the united Bâle Colour Works, and believe us,

> Dear Sir,
> Very sincerely Yours,
> Society of Chemical Industry in Bâle,
> J. R. Geigy S.A.
> Chemical Works, formerly Sandoz,
> Durand & Huguenin S.A."

From some of the signatories I had private letters too. The souvenir was a Patek-Philippe watch. It was all very gratifying! The Minister at Berne wrote in flattering terms to the Foreign Office of the "very heavy work" I had done at Bâle, and the Consul-General at Zurich, Sir Cecil Hertslet, who presided at a farewell dinner given to me, wrote home in the same strain and enclosed copy of the letter I have reproduced above. The reply he received was rather a surprise to him. It

expressed satisfaction at my work; but the sting of the wasp
was in the tail! He was "reminded, however," that it was
contrary to Foreign Office regulations for a Consular Officer
"to receive presents that might in any way be connected with
the discharge of his official duties."

"What do I do now? Give back the watch?" I asked
Hertslet the next time I saw him.

"Nonsense," he replied. "I have sent the FO a suitable
reply." Hertslet was rather good at sending suitable replies.
He had been our Consul-General at Antwerp until the German
invasion of Belgium.

On arrival in London my first calls were, of course, at the
Foreign Office. When I saw Lord Dufferin I said I was sorry
that I had involuntarily transgressed Consular regulations.

"My dear fellow," he said, "think no more about it. We
were all pleased to hear what Grant Duff and Hertslet told us,
and wrote to them to say so. Then some chap in the Second
Division dug up a regulation about bribery, so we added the
paragraph about the regulation having been broken. We are
ruled by Second Division clerks. Let's see the watch."

If the Second Division had only known, I had done more
than break a regulation. I had disobeyed a categorical instruction, but not in the matter of watches or bribes. A few weeks
after my arrival in Bâle an Englishman, George Pollitt, came
to see me. He told me very little about himself, beyond the
fact that he came from the War Office and had studied chemistry at the Zurich Polytechnic in the 1890's. I gathered later
that he was outstanding as a chemical scientist, worked for
Brunner Mond, and had joined the Army at the outbreak of
war as a despatch-riding motor cyclist. He was a fair-complexioned, no-nonsense Englishman, obviously full of drive.
His career in the Army was brilliant and I believe he was
largely instrumental in founding the ICI. But all that was
later. His manner was direct and he came to the point quickly.

"Will you do some work for the War Office?" he asked.

"What sort of work?"

"Well, you are sitting on the German frontier. You know

Switzerland, Germany, and the language. I think you could help us."

"Explain what I should be expected to do," I said. Pollitt explained.

"I've forgotten exactly how the FO worded it, and it's not worth getting out the despatch, which is safely locked away," I told him. "But the sense of the instruction is that I am forbidden to engage in anything which, in plain English, would be called spy-work. If I did and were discovered I would lose my job."

"And so?" inquired Pollitt.

"So I will do as you ask. The thing will be not to be found out."

On which, we went fully into the matter, the details of which are of no consequence now. They involved codes and contacts. In so far as the latter were human, my experience was and the impression remains with me, that many of them were impostors, and some of them knaves. There were some genuine ones, and I knew one who risked his life on more than one occasion in Germany. He was an Englishman. Another Englishman, who was supposed to be looking after things from Geneva, was an inflated fraud, a rich cushy, playing tennis and frequenting night clubs in order, as he said, to provide cover. This work cost me many tiring week-end visits to various Swiss towns; and there were visits to Paris—to our own people and to their colleagues in the French War Ministry—as well as to GHQ, Ypres and Poperinghe. Colonel Kirke, who was running the Intelligence Corps at GHQ, was grateful and encouraging when I protested that I was afraid the scraps of information I was able to feed to him from Bâle must be of little use. So was Colonel MacEwen who wrote to me in November, 1915, from the French War Ministry in Paris thanking me for "the very valuable notes" I had sent him. But my own view persists, that a vast amount of "spy" information is humbug and most of it quite unreliable.

One of the curious points about this whole spy business, as far as Switzerland was concerned, was that the professional spies were so seldom arrested by the Swiss authorities. I have an idea that the latter had a shrewd idea what humbugs most of them were. To make up for it, they occasionally arrested quite innocent people. I sometimes found soldiers posted at the door of my lodgings. I was never sure whether this was a prelude to my own arrest, or whether the authorities had knowledge (though not from me!) of some of the threats I had received from German patriots and decided I ought to be "protected". But they did one day arrest Fitzgerald Campbell, author and journalist, who was at that time working for *The Times*. He had called on me and we had had lunch together. He had come to Switzerland to "take the temperature" of Swiss neutrality before going to France as *The Times* war correspondent with the French armies. He was an attractive personality, a little over fifty years of age, as unassuming as he was brilliant. As I told our Consul-General, the Swiss refused to be specific as to why they had arrested him. However, Grant Duff made representations, and Campbell left for his assignment in France, which earned him several decorations.

Shortly before I left Bâle in January, 1916, I had reported to our Minister in Berne that the Germans were entrenching at St Ludwig, my surmise being that it did not look much as if there would be the German offensive in Alsace that had been predicted. But in the following February I had a letter from Mrs Corning, the wife of the very distinguished American professor of anatomy who was dean of the Medical Faculty at Bâle and wrote and lectured in German. I dined with them frequently at their home and we became friends. Mrs Corning's letter, which reached me in London, is a reminder how close Switzerland was to the fighting. "The cannon have been awful—never anything like it before and always the worst at night," she wrote. "The Alsatian villages up to the Auschwil frontier have all been evacuated. Fancy, if one walked out in 30 minutes to a *French* frontier, and said *bonjour* to a *poilu*! . . We like Mr Beak [my successor at Bâle] very much, and much better than at first. He seems more keen and awake now, and he is so scholarly and really awfully interesting about Africa."

In 1913 Rudolf Steiner, a German philosopher, had founded

154

n Anthroposophical Society and inveigled a number of men
nd women into building with their own hands a so-called
Temple of Peace, in which, apparently, to house his anthropo-
ophist teachings. The work continued despite the war. This
emple was just outside Bâle, and some English ladies were
mong the sprinkling of disciples who worshipped the author
f "How to arrive at Knowledge of the Higher Worlds," "Of
Soul Puzzles", and other mystical lucubrations. Some of these
adies came to me periodically to have their signatures
vitnessed on forms entitling them to receive some dividends
rom England. They had no compunction about working for
a German in war time. As far as I could make out, most of
heir money went to Steiner personally, while they nearly
tarved themselves to death.

Of two of these ladies Mrs Corning wrote to me after I left
Bâle: "Mrs R. and I see quite a lot of each other since you
eft. She is a quaint hermit person. And isn't it strange how
uddenly every one is Roman Catholic over here? Miss D. is
ather better; at least, she eats well and is physically better, but
s still quite off it. She has started a fiancé now (quite an
maginary person, who does not exist); but she writes to him
n the uncanniest way, and occasionally mistakes Professor
Wolff [one of Corning's colleagues in the Faculty] for her
'Ted.' They seem to be quite kind to her out there at the
'temple' camp. We have not been to the 'Confessional' since
you left; but the red lamp-shade can still be seen from the
road. Incidentally, it begins to feel quite time that you came
back again!"

The allusion is to a kind of occasional At Home instituted
by the little English group of Steiner adepts. I had nick-named
t The Confessional because, if one let the ladies ramble on,
the conversation smacked of a pseudo-psycho-spiritualist
session.

"*French*-Swiss troops are coming up here next week," wrote
Mrs Corning at the end of February, 1916. "In fact, only the
French-Swiss divisions are to be mobilized: odd, isn't it? The
Divisional Staff is to be at Arlesheim again, so we shall see
some life. Ursula [the Cornings' daughter of about 12] sends you

her latest naval riddles. She is much occupied tearing Iron
Crosses on the approved Hamblochian pattern!"

The "naval riddles" were:—

> When is a ship ambitiously in love?
> When she is making up to a pier.

> When is a ship contemptible in love?
> When she is anchoring after a swell.

> When is a ship foolishly in love?
> When she is attached to a buoy.

> When is a ship wisely in love?
> When she is tender to a man-o'-war.

Corning was a tall, spare man of about fifty, with an aquiline
nose over a bristly moustache. Keen eyes looked at one through
gold-rimmed spectacles; but the severe look could break into
pleasant smiles, and he had a great sense of humour.

One day he telephoned to me. I was booked to dine with
them at their house that evening.

"I have rung you up," he said, "to tell you that my colleague
Michaelis has invited himself to dinner this evening. His wife
went to Stuttgart unexpectedly this morning and won't be
back till tomorrow. It might embarrass you to meet him. How
do you feel about it?"

Michaelis was a German professor of whom I had often
heard Corning speak. I thought for a moment and then said

"That's all right. I should rather like to meet him, as I know
what a good opinion you have of him. If anybody knows
that I have dined at the same table as an enemy subject, my
reply will be that it was inevitable and on neutral territory."

It turned out to be a very pleasant evening. I knew from
Corning that Michaelis was a very liberal-minded man, and
we all of us found plenty of topics for conversation without
a single allusion to the war. There was no constraint.

An evening of real constraint was one when Corning enter-

tained at dinner an English lady married to a German who
had been a fellow-student of Corning's in Germany and was
now a professor at the Berlin University. Corning had warned
me that I should find this English lady more German than
any German *Hausfrau*. And so it was. Her hair was tightly
brushed back into a bun. She wore a very plain dress and had
a curiously pained look. I judged her to be about forty-five;
but she might have been any age. She had lived in Berlin ever
since her marriage and had never been back to England. She
spoke English haltingly and with a pronounced German
intonation, for German had clearly become her 'native' tongue.
It was obvious, too, that she was completely ignorant of all
that had been going on in the world outside Germany. I don't
think that in those days I had ever heard the word 'indoctrin-
ated,' but the lady was an example of its meaning. German ways
of thought and speech had become an exclusively pervading
influence; and it is not given to every English lady in such
circumstances to escape it by writing books like *Elizabeth
and her German Garden*.

I missed Corning's intellectual stimulus during my following,
long years in Brazil. We corresponded; but we were both
busy men, and our letters were not long. We never met again.
The other two American friends in my life, John Gordon,
the mining engineer and company director, and James
Woltman, the Standard Oil man, were keen-witted and
excellent company; but Corning's intellectual attainments
were of an exceptionally high order. In sagacity, however, the
three Americans were equals. All three married Englishwomen.

A letter I had from Grant Duff, our Minister at Berne,
shortly before I left Bâle is of some interest. After some kind
remarks on my "good promotion," he told me he had "brought
to the notice of the Federal Council" and was sending me a
copy of their "not very satisfactory reply" the case of a British
subject in Bâle, Crowe, who was a cousin of Sir Eyre Crowe at
the Foreign Office. Falconer Crowe had been summoned to the
office of the Chief of Police and warned to "discontinue his
spying activities." Crowe was a tubby, very voluble little
merchant who would not have had the faintest notion how even

to begin to be a spy. The war had brought him unlooked-for prosperity and he had been denounced by two commercial competitors, Swiss, who were jealous of my having entrusted to his firm, and not to them, the transport of the dye materials I have already spoken about.

Grant Duff's letter went on: "I wonder whether, if Crowe had a grievance, the Bâle police would act with such promptitude. . . . There seems lately to have been a regular set at British subjects here. One writes from prison to say he had already been confined 58 days without trial. This is the land of the much-boomed W. Tell!"

The disparaging "W. Tell" is delicious. As who should write "J. Caesar" or "N. Bonaparte."

No doubt it was because Dr Blocher, the Bâle Chief of Police, was such a thorough-going Marxist that he was devoid of humour and an ardent pro-German. But the *Basler Vorwärts*, the organ of the Bâle Socialist Party, was not without a sense of proportion. When at the end of November, 1915, the *Frankfurter Zeitung* published an editorial exalting the "immortally memorable" feat of German arms (with some very perfunctorily acknowledged help from Austria and Bulgaria) in crushing Serbia, the Swiss paper, on December 1st, published an ironical article under the heading "*Inflated Laurels*." I quote this as an instance that, though the Swiss may not have entertained any particularly warm feelings towards us, most of them were by no means pro-German.

It was self-evident, wrote the *Basler Vorwärts*, that Serbia was merely an excuse for Germany and Austria to embark on a war which should establish German hegemony in Europe. But, said the Swiss newspaper, if it had not been for the ravages of typhus in the Serbian army and for the treacherous unprovoked flank attack on Serbia by Bulgaria, even Mackensen's troops might not have got the better of the Serbs who had previously so completely routed the Austrians. All the "theatrical kissing between Kaisers William and Francis-Joseph in Vienna cannot change the real facts of this inglorious victory."

Chapter X

The United States: an informed opinion — War and the FO —
Parkinson's Law in Rio de Janeiro — Old Timers — Founding a
Chamber of Commerce — Buenos Aires and other journeys.

I N THE MATTER of influence private secretaries to the Secretary of State for Foreign Affairs are like Tom Wessels, the public house proprietor in Kipling's tale about the *Archimandrite*, in being "persons of influence beyond Admirals." Shortly after I arrived in London in February, 1916, on my way from Bâle to Rio de Janeiro, I was told that Sir William (later Baron) Tyrrell, who was then Private Secretary to Sir Edward Grey, wanted to see me at his flat in town where he was recovering from influenza. I was to meet Hugh Spender who at that time was Diplomatic Correspondent for the *Westminster Gazette*. They wanted to question me about Switzerland and the Swiss in war time. I went and they did so. But from my point of view the interesting part of the interview was listening to Spender talking on the United States and the Americans. He had just returned from New York and was full of the subject. The United States were 'nootral,' though not quite in the manner presented in a *Punch* drawing where an American in a London club was saying very pleasantly: "Of course, we're neutral. We don't care which of you Allies licks the Kaiser."

Spender pointed out that people in England started off on the wrong foot when they spoke of Americans as "our cousins" and lulled themselves into thinking that the "ties of blood" were so strong that the people of the United States were bound to be "on our side." The so-called ties of blood, said Spender, were worth nothing; and in any case were largely imaginary.

In brief Spender's views were as follows, and I give them

because I believe them to be applicable today:— He agreed emphatically when I said I thought that we should avoid a great deal of misunderstanding if we regarded them as a foreign country. In practice we do not do so. In Whitaker's Almanack, for instance, information about the world's countries begins, quite understandably, with the United Kingdom. Next come Commonwealth countries, followed by the United States. Then comes a large heading: Foreign Countries, under which such countries are dealt with in alphabetical order. But is not the United States a foreign country? If not, what is it? A Special Relation? And if so, what is a Special Relation?

The ties-of-blood argument was a delusion, said Spender, because only 25 per cent of the inhabitants of the United States were of British descent. Immigrants from every country in the world were in the majority as ancestors of the American nation. These people and their offspring felt no affection for the British people. There was no reason why they should; and, in any case American history books had taught them to believe that the English, headed by King George III and his Ministers, had been tyrannical enemies of American liberty. There were, moreover, millions of people of German descent hostile to the British, while descendants of Italians, Poles, Scandinavians, and other peoples had no reason to feel particularly friendly towards the British.

To counterbalance all this, however, three of the best things the Americans had and treasured were inherited from the British: constitutional government; independence of the courts of law (from the executive); and freedom of the Press. In these three directions there were, according to Spender, links with Great Britain; but the links were purely historical, intellectual, and incidental. Similarly in the matter of language. None of these links constituted any political identity of views. Indeed, Great Britain and the United States in their political aims, to say nothing of their commercial rivalries, were as much opposed to each other as any two nations could be. It was in our interest to win the United States to our side in the war. It was self-interest which might, as we hoped, persuade them to become our allies.

The FO was a changed place. The assistant under-secretaries and senior clerks sat in solitary state in the noble rooms; but other rooms and corridors were now cluttered up with desks and their occupants. There was much bustle and there were many visitors, most of them business men wanting to see some official or other in the Commercial and Sanitary Department. Why "sanitary" I never discovered. Its Controller was Algernon Law, under whom I had already worked for a short time when I joined the Service. I found him as competent and caustic as ever. Other smaller sectional divisions had been invented for "war work". The men who staffed them sat behind screens that partitioned off the ball-room into sections, and the two or three men thus segregated dealt with matters like contraband, raw materials wanted for war purposes, and a host of similar problems, but a full-blown new department had been created: it was called the Foreign Trade Department and was run by Roland Nugent, a man of my own age.

Nugent was destined to become Leader and then Speaker of the Northern Ireland Senate, after spending some years as Director of the Federation of British Industries. But in 1915 and 1916 he was industriously tackling commercial questions, of which he had never had any practical experience, and tackling them well, so well that the founders of the FBI made it worth his while to throw up his career in the Foreign Office and join them. Guy Locock, with whom I had worked in the Foreign Office, was another to be lured away by the FBI. When war broke out (1914) he was Private Secretary to Francis Acland, Parliamentary Under Secretary at the F.O. In quick, almost impatient, penetration of the essential of any subject Locock was a contrast to Nugent who was painstaking rather than brilliant. Both men were efficient. But while Nugent gave one the impression of being weighed down by the seriousness of his job, Locock would enlighten any problem with a quip and a smile.

As far as my end of the world—Brazil—was concerned, what was bothering Nugent was that the Germans were so well dug in commercially all over Brazil, and not least in the

L

Amazon river ports. The Bishop of Santarém, for instance, was an ex-Prussian Guards officer, though that is, of course, ecclesiastical rather than commercial penetration. The immediate task was to try and stop Brazilian products being shipped to Germany through neutral countries in Europe, more especially Sweden. We were only partially successful in preventing this. Swedish merchants must have made a mint of money out of the First World War, importing coffee, rubber, vegetable oils and other Brazilian products far in excess of their own country's capacity of consumption.

What with conferences at the Foreign Office and visits to firms in the City having connexions in Brazil, I was really tired when I embarked on the Royal Mail *Demerara* for Brazil. One thing I had found unsatisfactory. It was that the FO, having invented the job of Commercial Attaché to the British Legation in Brazil, seemed to have no idea of what they wanted him to do. When I pressed Algernon Law on the subject, he said airily: "Oh, you have *carte blanche*." Which was gratifying personally, but professionally vague. Ten months after my arrival in Brazil I did receive a despatch with some nebulous "instructions." But I had already marked out my own line of work.

Petropolis is a delightful residence. It is 2,500 ft above sea level, in a wooded gap in the Organ Mountains that form the impressive drop-curtain at the head of the Bay of Rio de Janeiro. Brazil's second emperor, Dom Pedro, after whom it is named, chose it as his residence during the summer months, when the heat in Rio can be very trying. Foreign envoys naturally followed the Court, and the custom continued in republican days. The President of the Republic and his Cabinet ministers lived at Petropolis from October 31, the eve of All Saint's day, until the Rio Carnival folly had subsided, usually by the end of the following March. In practice, however, the time spent by Government officials in Petropolis became gradually shorter. Rio was becoming a pleasant place to live in even during the heat, and Petropolis was far too remote for the transaction of business, even government business. Most foreign Legations had begun to have their permanent official residences in Rio, the Petropolis jaunt being considered rather in the light of a summer holiday when envoys and their staff rented houses or apartments for a few weeks, or lived in the only real hotel, which was run by an Austrian lady, a widow. Our own Government, on the other hand, having bought a bungalow residence at a bargain price (£15,000), the seller having no idea that the buyer was merely a man of straw for the British authorities, made Petropolis the domicile of the Legation, our Minister coming down to Rio for a few months in the cooler weather and either living in an hotel or renting an apartment. It was a very unsatisfactory arrangement. The Minister wasted much time travelling backwards and forwards from Petropolis, since the people he wanted to see were in Rio; and he was out of touch with things in general.

Between the wars the FO decided that our Embassy should be located in Rio de Janeiro. An official from the Office of Works came out and a house was bought that a local broker was longing to get rid of because the municipal authorities were going to drive a new road through his property and his compensation would have been small. For years the house stood empty. I called it Bleak House, and the joke was not appreciated. However, eventually our authorities in Whitehall, having acquired the habit of thinking in millions, decided to get rid of Bleak House and go the whole hog. They spent £1,000,000 or rather more on building an Embassy, in which incidentally the architect had forgotten to allow for enough rooms. A new Embassy in Brasília will probably cost £2,000,000.

Is all this really necessary? In the early 1900's British exporters were Brazil's most important suppliers, filling nearly 50 per cent of Brazil's import requirements. Today, we are among the Also Ran as exporters to Brazil. In other words, the expense of Embassy buildings and staff is in inverse ratio to our trade with Brazil. Even during the hectic 1914–18 war years the Legation staff never exceeded four:— The Minister, one First Secretary, a Commercial Attaché (myself), and an archivist.

By 1966 the Embassy staff was eighteen:— The Ambassador, a Minister, two (!) Counsellors, four First Secretaries, four Second Secretaries, and among other lesser lights a Veterinary Attaché. Supernumerary clerks and typists are not included in these figures. All this array of minute-writers in a country with which we have no frontier questions (not even a Falkland Islands problem!) and no political problems, a country in which our share in its economic development is relatively negligible. However, for good measure, the British taxpayer also maintains a British Council office with a staff of six in Rio de Janeiro, and subsidizes visits—official tourism—of scores of Brazilians to this country every year. Parkinson's Law is in full force in the matter of Anglo-Brazilian relations in this year of grace (and favour) and balance-of-payments difficulties.

When I arrived back in Rio early in 1916 it was quite obvious to me that if I was to do any worthwhile work, I could not do it in the pleasant little mountain resort of Petropolis. None of the Cabinet ministers lived there, and only a handful of business men stayed there. Rio's yellow fever days were a thing of the past. Copacabana had grown from a few fisher-men's huts, as I had known it in 1910, to a sea-side suburb, and Rio's other suburbs were quite as pleasant and more healthy. Petropolis was really an anachronism. It took over two hours to get there by rail; and there was no motor road then.

Sir Arthur Peel, our Minister (1915–19), was quite under-standing. He was a bachelor. It was agreed that I should get an office in Rio and we would meet when Peel came down from Petropolis to call on a Minister, and occasionally I would go up to Petropolis. By today's standards we were much under-staffed. As for my own work, I had no staff at all. I worked throughout the war as a "unit of one". Which was, of course, very foolish of me. I should have bombarded the FO for help. I had hardly got installed in my office when I found myself giving accommodation to a Naval attaché, a Convoy admiral, a Marine GSO and the staff that they insisted the Admiralty should authorize them to engage. In any case, we all got on well together, and as they spoke nothing but English they found it convenient to have me at hand.

"I am here to represent my Government to the Brazilian Government," Sir Arthur Peel was saying to me one day when I was staying with him at Petropolis. Two British community societies differed over some trivial point of interpretation of rules for sending home donations to war charities, and had asked Peel to decide between them. "I am not going to be bothered with their squabbles," went on Peel. "Of course, I will go to any function of theirs when my presence is appropriate. But why on earth don't they take their troubles to the Consul-General? He is the head of the community."

I didn't reply to that question, though I knew the answer. What I did say was that from my own experience in charge of the Consulate-General the British community's interests had always seemed to me to be too widely dispersed, and the war had produced even more societies and associations.

Peel at once suggested that I could do something to harmonize things. I demurred. What I should have done was honestly plead over-work; but I never did that during my time as a Government official. I told Peel I could hardly approach leading members of the community over the Consul-General's head. "Oh, get him to co-operate," said Peel airily, and then added flatteringly: "They listened to you when you put the Chamber of Commerce idea to them. Why shouldn't they do so now?" In a weak moment I yielded. There were in Rio at that time various British clubs, mostly for sport; and there were a number of do-good societies, a British Library, a Church committee, a Seamen's Mission, a Seamen's Hospital which I had been instrumental in founding when I was Acting Consul-General; and the war had brought into operation a Red Cross Society and several other associations.

I got the committees of all these various clubs and associations to meet me, but nothing that I could say would persuade them to pool their activities. Nor was I any more successful when we hired a hall and held a meeting of the whole community. But there was one little speech which made a great impression on me. It was the custom for the societies I have mentioned to get up dances and fêtes, where drinks flowed freely and there was much merriment. The entrance fees went to whatever charity the society that organized the festivity was interested in. Tom Cross, a British business man whose son was at the Front, rose and said: "The idea seems to be that without *festas* and dances, money will not be forthcoming for war charities. Personally, I don't believe it. But," he went on, speaking with great emotion, "if these dances continue to be held to raise funds, then I want to see something done to bring home to people what they are dancing for. Let the dancing be interrupted while a screen is lowered and on it are projected some of the horrors of war—the trenches, the mud, the barbed wire, the wounded, the shelling: in short, something of what this war really means to our brave lads, our sons or brothers, who are being mutilated or killed while we dance."

There was a pained and, as it seemed to me, almost guilty silence when Tom Cross sat down. No one backed his suggestion; in fact no one said anything. Any idea of pooling activities was dead. I proposed we adjourn the meeting. There was nothing more to be said. The Old Timers had won.

As a matter of interest the idea that the British community in Rio de Janeiro should at least have a common meeting place, if not a home, did occur. The Prefect of Rio de Janeiro, Dr Carlos Sampaio, in some of the talks I had with him in preparation for our participation in the Brazilian Centenary Exhibition of 1922, proposed that a new building should be erected in Rio de Janeiro, the greater part of the cost to be defrayed by the Prefecture. Great Britain, on her part, would contribute the rest of the cost and the building would house the majority of British offices in Rio; there would be shops too, and rooms for social occasions. The whole building would be called *Casa Britânica*. I passed the idea on to Whitehall and to the recently formed British Chamber of Commerce in Brazil. But I felt pretty sure there would be no enthusiasm. There wasn't; and I had to tell the Prefect so.

As Peel had said, I had been successful in establishing a British Chamber of Commerce in Brazil. But only after much hard work. When I came to London after leaving Bâle and called on people in the city, heads of firms with business connexions in Brazil had expressed polite interest, rarely more, while the senior partner of a London merchant bank was positively hostile. When I asked him what his real objection was, his reply was: "You can't expect us to give away to others the fruits of our business experience in Brazil which extends over the past seventy years."

"I believe you are members of the London Chamber of Commerce," I said.

"Yes," he replied.

"Well, I may assume that you don't on that account give away to anybody something you want to keep to yourselves. In any case," I added, "I shall go ahead with my idea, and once I get the Chamber started, I feel sure that your firm will be applying for membership." Which is what happened.

In my round of visits to British firms in Rio de Janeiro I found no positive objections, merely an attitude on the part of most managers of "I don't see what good a Chamber of Commerce would do us." However, when I called a meeting of the community on August 11, 1916, and made a speech and answered many questions, there was a unanimous vote in favour of the idea, and two months later, after much work drafting articles of association, the scheme was successfully launched. The British community in São Paulo did not fall in with my suggestion that they should join forces with Rio de Janeiro. They preferred to form their own Chamber.

One of the most interesting sequels to the foundation of the British Chambers of Commerce in Brazil was a visit I received from the United States Consul. He told me that American business men in Rio de Janeiro had been following with great attention what I had been doing, and he had been instructed to approach me for hints on how to establish an American Chamber of Commerce. The Americans were quick to imitate, and their organization flourishes today.

I was flattered to be asked to be the first chairman of our Chamber, but declined. Chambers must be free and independent of Government officials. So I was elected an honorary life member.

Of my travels up and down Brazil, more especially in the

North, during the 1914-18 War I have written in *British Consul*. In my journey south I went first to Buenos Aires. On the steamer was a Mr Brancker, brother of the famous soldier-airman. He was a director of one of the big British meat importers from the Argentine and was going there on business. He invited me to meet Lady Curzon at dinner at his hotel in Buenos Aires. Lady Curzon was the daughter of a United States diplomatist, J. Monroe Hinds, who had been Minister to Brazil. By her first husband, Alfred Duggan, Lady Curzon had children over whose inheritance there was a complicated legal dispute. Were they Argentine or United States citizens? Lady Curzon had come out to try and get the dispute settled. The Marquess of Curzon was at that time (1917) Lord President of the Council, so that Lady Curzon had *les petites* and *les grandes entrées* wherever she went. In her own right, however, she could dispense with them for she was a strikingly handsome woman of great charm. It was evident that Brancker was under her spell. Some months later Lady Curzon stopped at Rio de Janeiro on her way to England and attended a ball given by the Brazilian Foreign Minister. Edwin Morgan, the American Ambassador, danced assiduously with her; but I don't think he ever fell under any woman's spell.

Morgan was a very puffy-faced bachelor, who drove about Rio in a Tin Lizzie on the doors of which were painted the United States coat of arms. His chauffeur was a giant of a man, who seemed to treat his master with disdain. For many years Morgan was the only foreign diplomatist of ambassadorial rank. That meant that he could always break the queue of any of his colleagues who happened to be waiting to see the Minister of Foreign Affairs. His walk was Agag-like, and he was known by many as Pussy-foot. He was soft-spoken, and his manner was always courteous.

Naturally I called to pay my respects to our Minister when I was in Buenos Aires. He was Sir Reginald Tower—a bachelor, like Peel and Morgan. I was warned before I called that I should probably find him in company with a parrot. A parrot was indeed walking about freely over books and papers while we talked, and I wondered whether the consequences of such freedom were not at times disastrous. Presumably Tower wanted the bird for company. I knew a lady in England who had a parrot loose in her drawing-room. She would sometimes draw it to her and kiss its nozzle. Her own nose was exactly like a parrot's beak, so I assumed that in some previous existence she had been a parrot. But Tower was nothing like a parrot. He was tall and thin, had a short beard and wore spectacles. His appearance was donnish. His parrot did not squawk, at least not when I was with him.

I crossed by boat to Montevideo and remembered that the owner of the steamship line was the friend of a Croatian peasant I had met at Ragusa. His name was Mihanovitch and his story is worth re-telling. In the 1880's he had been a stoker on a British steamer that called at Buenos Aires. Mihanovitch went on shore and liked the place. On his return he asked the captain to pay him off. This the captain refused to do, as the stoker had signed on for the round voyage. Mihanovitch said nothing, but a few days later, when the ship was a mile from port on her homeward voyage, he jumped overboard and swam to shore. In his mouth he carried his whole capital: one golden sovereign. Within a few years he owned one of the most flourishing Argentine shipping lines.

In Buenos Aires I lunched with our Minister, Mitchell Innes, who struck me as austerely monastic though married. I then called on the manager of the British railway by which I proposed to travel northwards to Rio Grande do Sul, across Uruguay. I had been warned that he was a pillar of the local Anglican Church, of which he was a churchwarden, and that he was very strait-laced. I found him pleasant enough, though rather pompous: a tall, rather heavily-built man, with a flowing fair moustache. His reputation for extreme respectability seemed enhanced by the fact that he wore a black frock coat. This was certainly old fashioned. Curiously enough, a few days later, I found that our Consul at Pôrto Alegre, Dillon, an Irishman, wore one too, and a top hat into the bargain when he took his walks abroad. Indeed in his case it was really a case of "trailing his coat." He asked me to walk with him down a street called

Voluntários da Pátria, which was where most of the many German firms in Pôrto Alegre had their stores and offices. It was a very hot afternoon, so he substituted a large panama for his top hat. He buttoned his frock coat tightly round his ample body, so that the shape of a large revolver which he stuck in the hip pocket of his white trousers was clearly visible.

"I do this nearly every day," Dillon confided to me, as we walked slowly down the street.

"Do you think it does any good?" I asked.

"I don't know," he replied. "But there are lots of these Germans here, and they're very cocky. Are sure they are winning the war, and I think it does them good to see we are not afraid of them."

"I am sure it does you good," I said. Dillon was a dentist by profession; but his Consular job during the war took up all his time, and he did excellent, conscientious work for us.

But to return to the railway manager. A few years later, the very sedate and strait-laced man I had met in Montevideo came to Brazil to manage a British railway. Within a few months the transformation of the man reminded me of the old music-hall song:

> Oh Flo', what a change, you know,
> When she left the village she was shy.
> But alas and alack,
> She came back,
> With a naughty little twinkle in her eye.

He shaved off his moustache, and no longer wore a frock coat but a white suit. His complexion grew ruddy; he lived a gay bachelor life, became a *bon viveur* and, after a few short years, paid the penalty by having a fatal stroke.

I was glad not to have lost touch with the Foreign Office altogether, though it was the newly created hybrid Department of Overseas Trade that got most of the reports I sent home. In any case, Peel was asked to "convey to Mr Hambloch" the Foreign Secretary's "thanks for his valuable and interesting report on political and trade conditions in the three Southern

States of Brazil." Then I went north through all the other States of Brazil, and the Council of the Chamber in Rio gave me a "complimentary banquet" on my return "after a prolonged tour in the North of Brazil." It was all very gratifying; but I was doing far too much. I had been laid low with fever for six weeks in Manaus, and my health was never robust afterwards.

Chapter XI

The DOT and other trials — The De Bunsen Mission to Brazil —
Founding the FBI — Bringing a Brazilian Delegation to England
— A President-elect in London —Real Tears — Dinner in the House
of Commons — Lloyd George in Rio de Janeiro.

I WAS TO PASS the next twenty years in Brazil, thirteen of
them in Government service; and I often recalled what
Sir Beethom Whitehead had said to me when I served
under him at Belgrade and was offered a choice of posts:
"If you choose Brazil and do well there, they'll keep you there."
But "they"—HM Government—were not wholly responsible.
It was I who elected to stay on there when I left the Service.

With one exception (and he, poor chap, became a mental
case) I found all my Legation and Embassy colleagues pleasant
to work with. I always had my own office and during the War
(1914-18) worked single-handed. In 1919, I was given an
allowance for office help, but had, most unwillingly, to transfer
my allegiance from the Foreign Office to the Department of
Overseas Trade. This hybrid department was generated in the
autumn of 1917. It was the offspring of the FO and the Board
of Trade, but neither of them recognized parental responsibility for it. It was a convenient dumping ground for misfits.
It was recruited largely from Second Division subaltern
employees in other Government offices in London who found
in the DOT a heaven-sent chance of increased pay and easily
acquired promotion. As the new Department was specifically
created for "promoting and developing British trade abroad,"
it was perhaps only to be expected that few, if any, of the junior
Class II civil servants who had leapt into Class I posts in the
newly created department would have the slightest knowledge

of trade, much less any experience of overseas trade, or indeed any acquaintance with a foreign country or language.

A mission was sent by the British Government to Brazil early in 1918. Its object was to convey to the Brazilian Government our satisfaction at Brazil's having (on October 26, 1917) declared war on Germany. It was late in the day, but Brazil was the only Latin American country to join the Allies and it was thought fitting that our appreciation should be conveyed with all pomp and ceremony.

The Foreign Office and our Minister, Sir Arthur Peel, between them had decided that an act well calculated to show our appreciation would be to raise the status of our diplomatic representation in Brazil from Legation to Embassy. Peel hoped to be our first Ambassador. It should be recalled that all this was at a time (in the years preceding 1918) when to be an Ambassador was a real distinction. We had only nine embassies: in Paris, Berlin, Vienna, Rome, St Petersburg, Tokio, Washington, Constantinople, and Madrid. In twenty-six other world capitals we had Legations; and there were chargés d'affaires or ministers resident in some other countries.

It was not, however, because Peel was a bachelor that he did not get the promotion to Ambassador. At least twelve colleagues of his in the Service were senior to him, and the heads of the Foreign Office were anxious to send one of their very best men to the new post. That is why they chose Sir Ralph Paget, who was quite an outstanding diplomatist in every way.

The Mission that came to Brazil early in 1918 was headed by Sir Maurice de Bunsen, who had been our Ambassador in Vienna until the outbreak of war in 1914. It was from him that I had received, at Ragusa after some delays, the regulation telegram "War declared". Whereupon I proceeded to burn cyphers and other confidential papers and nearly set my flat alight.

The other members of the De Bunsen Mission consisted of an admiral, keen, very active, and austere; a general, apparently neither keen nor active, and certainly not austere; a Member of Parliament (Sir) James A. Grant, only mildly interested, I found, in the Brazilian political scene, but concerned with how best to bring home to Brazilians, if possible, how great were the sacrifices being made by the British nation in the war; a business man, Follett Holt, who was chairman of several British companies with large investments in Brazil and Argentina; and W. S. Barclay, who had done some travelling in South America and written a book about it. A young Foreign Office man was De Bunsen's secretary.

De Bunsen made pleasant speeches, in which Canning's name recurred frequently and suitably; the admiral looked at Brazilian ships; the general looked at pretty women; the business man looked after the interests of his companies; and the travelled author stored up more impressions of South America. There were excursions, banquets, speeches, a visit to São Paulo, garden parties and receptions. The visit was declared a great success. I don't know that it achieved much, or indeed anything. But it was a gesture. I asked Barclay how they had spent their time on board ship coming out. He told me they had had one or two conferences, but nothing like a plan of action for the Mission had emerged. I said that De Bunsen, with his erect figure, trim white beard, and courteous manner seemed outwardly at any rate to look the part of ambassador. Barclay smiled.

"Do you know how Follett Holt describes him?" he said. "'Solid marble from the shoulders up.'" A quite unmerited sneer, I think.

Be that as it may, De Bunsen went down very well with the Brazilians. There was an amusing incident as far as I was personally concerned. At a Brazilian Foreign Office reception, the Minister of Foreign Affairs, Dr Nilo Peçanha, whom I knew quite well, whispered in my ear: "I have sung your praises to His Excellency De Bunsen." I thanked him, but was really surprised when De Bunsen told me later that the Minister had actually done so.

The De Bunsen Mission was housed in the Guanabara Palace, Rio de Janeiro, originally built for Princess Isabel, daughter of Dom Pedro II and Regent during his absences in Europe. It had been restored in 1908 for the National Exhibition of that year. It looked like an exhibition building—a mixture of rococo and wedding cake. It is pleasantly situated in beautiful grounds and has traditionally served to house distinguished visitors like King Albert I of Belgium and a President of Portugal.

In 1916—incidentally the year in which I had succeeded in bringing into being the British Chamber of Commerce in Brazil—a prominent business man, Mr Frank Dudley Docker, founded the Federation of British Industries. Of course, he did not do it single-handed; but he was, quite rightly I believe, regarded as the founder; indeed, he was proclaimed to be so by the Federation's first representative abroad, P. J. McKellen, who came to Brazil in 1919.

In its earliest days men like Sir Peter Rylands, Sir Richard Vassar-Smith, Sir Robert Hadfield, Sir Herbert Dixon, Lord Aberconway, Sir Algernon Firth, Sir Vincent Caillard, and Sir E. Manville were among the Federation's presidents and vice-presidents. No doubt, they with others collaborated in founding the FBI. But McKellen assured me that the original idea and impetus came from Dudley Docker.

The FBI administrators soon turned their minds to overseas trade. The first move they made in this direction was just after the war ended (in November, 1918). They decided to invite a delegation of Brazilian business men to visit Great Britain and be shown something of the country's industrial equipment and processes.

The first I knew of this was an instruction from the DOT, informing me that the FBI wanted to invite a Brazilian delegation composed of eight members in all. The leader would be appointed by the Brazilian Government; the other seven were, in effect, to be chosen by me.

The Versailles Peace Conference of 1919 was in full spate. Brazil's representative at it was an eminent jurisconsult, Dr Epitácio Pessoa, whose second-in-command was Dr Pandiá Calôgeras, an expert in financial and economic affairs. The Brazilian *políticos* chose Epitácio Pessoa as President, and Calôgeras was appointed to head the Brazilian Commercial Delegation that was to tour Great Britain at the invitation of the FBI.

João Pandiá Calôgeras was a remarkable man—engineer, politician, and historian. He was the son of a Greek father, an historian and educationist, who had come to Brazil in 1841, become a naturalized Brazilian, and was employed by the Monarchy. The son, João Pandiá, was born in Rio de Janeiro in 1870, when his father was sixty years of age. The Calôgeras family always spoke English at home, and Pandiá spoke it without an accent. During the FBI tour in Great Britain he made a number of speeches, always without notes and usually with a nice turn of wit. When we visited Parsons Marine Steam Turbine works at Newcastle, Sir C. Parsons presided at a lunch given by the firm, and in a speech of welcome spoke of radium, the possibilities of new sources of power, electric smelting, and so on. Calôgeras in his reply saluted Parsons as a poet—much to everybody's astonishment, until he went on to explain that Sir Charles Parson's outstanding position as an inventive worker was best defined by calling him a poet. The Greeks, he pointed out, used the same word, poet, for the man who put beautiful dreams into words and the man who converted scientific dreams into realities. Both were workers. Both *did* things. Therefore both were poets.

There was only one occasion when Calôgeras had a prepared speech in his pocket. It was one that was never delivered, for there were no speeches. The occasion was a lunch at New Court offered by the House of Rothschild, who had been bankers and loan issuers for the Brazilian Government since the days of the Brazilian Empire. To convey us from our hotel, the Savoy, to the luncheon, the FBI had ordered very long and large limousines. St Swithin's Lane is not one of London's widest thoroughfares and those who built the entrance to New Court in 1804 had not foreseen the arrival of large motor cars. Barclay was one of the party in my car, and as the chauffeur backed and edged forward and backed again before he could negotiate the narrow entrance, Barclay turned to me and said: "There seems to be a text in the Bible that would fit our case." "Yes," I said. "The eye of the needle, the camel, and the rich man."

In the matter of speeches and finance, the President-elect, Dr Epitácio Pessoa, when he came to London a few days later and was entertained at the Mansion House by the Lord Mayor, chided British financiers for not putting more money into Brazil. Seeing that just before the war (1914) a funding loan of over £14½ m. had been raised in London by Rothschild's to bolster Brazil's finances, the presidential censure fell rather flat. At the moment, of course, Epitácio Pessoa was feeling very sure of himself, more especially as his elevation to the presidency was as unexpected by him as it was by the Brazilian people. Brazil had accumulated considerable credits by shipping supplies to the Allies during the war, and he had received private assurances of loans from the United States, which, incidentally, never lent a cent to Brazil before 1921. Epitácio Pessoa had the reputation of being a good lawyer; but he was a bad administrator, and as President of the Republic he initiated an orgy of wasteful spending, so that when he quitted office in November, 1922, Brazil's finances were in a really parlous condition.

Directly the Commercial Delegation had completed its FBI tour, the new President appointed Calôgeras Minister of War. This was the first Brazilian experiment of having a civilian for that post. Calôgeras was the best War Minister Republican Brazil ever had. But the experiment was never repeated. The Military were too jealous, and civilian presidents in Brazil have to rely on friendly generals to maintain them in power.

I had known Calôgeras when I was Acting Consul-General in Rio. He was then Minister of Finance. Herbert Moses, life president of the Brazilian Press Association, who was then Secretary of the Rio Commercial Association, wanted me to go with him to see the Minister about some Customs question that might affect British and other foreign imports. Calôgeras was not receiving anybody on the day we called. "It is impossible to see His Excellency," the secretaries told us. But there are always ways of turning the impossible into possible in Brazil. We climbed many back stairs to a small room on the top floor of the Ministry, and found Calôgeras sitting at an open window in his shirt-sleeves working hard at some statistics. He was a glutton for work.

I don't know that Moses and I were very successful in what

M

we hoped to achieve; but I think Calôgeras was amused that we
had, so to speak, run him to earth. He was a short man with
black hair and a black moustache which he trimmed Kaiser-
wise. This gave him rather a cocky air. His nose was large and
aquiline; and small, black eyes and thin lips contributed to
making him look rather formidable. The heels of his shoes
were raised to give him a couple of inches more height. Even
so, he was shorter than his wife, a stately lady.

The ship that brought the Brazilian delegation to England
arrived five days late, so that we had no time for settling down,
but were at once plunged into factory visits and festivities.
Thus, on the very first evening of our arrival we were taken to the
Royalty Theatre to see Somerset Maugham's play *Caesar's
Wife*. The Brazilian delegates were much impressed with the
acting. At one point Madame Brito, who was sitting next to me,
whispered: "She is shedding real tears." The reference was to
Fay Compton. Two days later, after a busy morning, we went
to the opening of the Military Tournament. My Brazilian
friends were delighted to see the King and Queen; but it was
clear from their comments among themselves that what really
pleased them was the chance to see Marshal Joffre and Admiral
Beatty who were in the Royal Box too.

To round off a full day the FBI had booked seats at the
Winter Garden Theatre that evening for *Kissing Time*, and
though the delegates had little English, Leslie Henson easily
got over any language barrier and made them laugh un-
restrainedly.

The FBI really did things on a lavish scale—as lavish as
post-war conditions would permit. There was no lack of
entertainment; there were pleasant days in the Trossachs;
there was a typically bitter cold June day in Buxton; and the
FBI officials attached to the tour even found time on occasions
to pilot the ladies on shopping expeditions while their husbands
were inspecting steel tubes or condensing plants. The FBI
certainly deserved full marks for their organization and
imagination, and the delegates were loud in their praises.

I must not omit to mention a sad case of indigestion. The
delegate from Northern Brazil, José Adonias, had brought

with him a young relative as his secretary. He was nineteen years of age and it was his first visit to Europe. During the tour this dark-haired, olive-skinned young Brazilian must have swallowed gallons of tea—hence the indigestion. He would go into a Lyons tea shop, order tea, and sit for hours transfixed, lost in admiration of the fair-haired waitresses. It was silent admiration, for he had not a word of English. He was decidedly of those who prefer blondes, several years before Miss Loos thought of mentioning this masculine propensity in the title of a book.

Dinner in the House of Commons was, of course, quite an event. It was given by the chairman of the St John del Rey Mining Company, which owned in Brazil the deepest gold mine in the world.

That the Brazilians might complete their education of the British way of life, there was a railway strike while we were at York and a coal strike while we were at Bradford. At the hotel in York the delegates were much intrigued at seeing large two-tiered glass bowls with a flame underneath placed in front of some of the guests of the hotel after lunch.

"What are they for?" I was asked.

I explained that they were for percolating coffee and were often used by people in England who thought they knew something about coffee. This caused my Brazilian friends much astonishment, for such contraptions were unknown in the largest coffee-producing country in the world. There are, of course, far simpler and more efficient ways of making a perfect cup of coffee. What really amused the Brazilians, I think, was the rapt attention with which the coffee-worshippers gazed at the glass erection in front of them, as though at a crystal ball.

Nottingham, for historical reasons and apart from lace and chemicals, was one of the places which the visitors from Brazil found particularly interesting, not least because of the existence in the neighbourhood of the reputedly oldest licensed house in the British Isles, "The Trip to Jerusalem," cut into a rock in 1199 and presumably used as a place of assembly for people from that part of the country joining the Crusades.

I told Aubrey Edgcumbe at the DOT that the delegates

would think their visit to Great Britain really complete if they could each go back to Brazil with a signed photograph of Lloyd George. Edgcumbe managed this successfully, as he seemed to manage everything that he had a hand in.

In the 1930's Lloyd George came to Brazil. I was no longer in the Service, but the Ambassador, Sir Beilby Alston, sought me out and asked if I would ghost something for Lloyd George who, in a speech he was to make, wanted to make some allusion to the circumstances which had caused Brazil to join the Allies in 1917. I gave the bald facts only. He could twist them as he liked for his speech.

Chapter XII

Another Marie Celeste — *Turkey and the* 1918 *Armistice* — *The Levant and Palestine* — *Our first Ambassador to Brazil* — *Some distinguished and other visitors.*

IN THE FIRST WORLD WAR large shipments of manganese were made from Brazil to the United States. The American Consul-General in Rio de Janeiro at that time was a man named Gottschalk. He was a pleasant man who knew how to make friends, but had a kind of additional popularity through being the grand-nephew of Louis-Moreau Gottschalk. This American composer and pianist was born in New Orleans and died in Rio de Janeiro. Among a number of exotic pieces he composed was a Fantasia on Motives from the Brazilian national anthem. This is an elaborate composition based on the original work of Francisco Manoel, itself quite an intricate piece of music and very long. When I took the Brazilian commercial delegates to England as guests of the FBI, we went to an evening's entertainment at Bellevue in Manchester. The management had so arranged things that directly the delegates appeared in the box reserved for them, the Brazilian national anthem should be played. On the floor of the house couples were dancing when we arrived. The music stopped, and after a slight pause the orchestra struck up the opening bars of the Brazilian national anthem. The dancers stopped and looked up at the "royal" box where the Brazilians were standing to attention. The piece is inordinately long, but has a swinging lilt; and presently one couple and then another and eventually the whole floor was dancing until the last note was played, when they all clapped. The Brazilians enjoyed the whole thing immensely. They said it was the first time people had danced to their national anthem. Gottschalk's fantasia is another matter. It is far longer, and of course far more ornate: in fact, a bravura piece for a concert pianist.

Now to come back to the American Consul Gottschalk, the composer's grand-nephew. During the First World War the *Cyclops*, an American transport ship, came to Brazil bringing coal and provisions for the United States fleet that was on patrol duty in the South Atlantic. For her return journey to the United States she loaded 15,000 tons of manganese. She was armed as an auxiliary cruiser and the American admiral sent her to Bahia to pick up 600 American sailors due for leave from the ships of his fleet. She did so and sailed north. As far as Barbados the *Cyclops* maintained contact with the shore and the American fleet. But after that, there was complete silence. Nothing more was heard from her. A minute search was carried out in West Indian waters and the Gulf of Mexico. Nothing was found; not a spar, not an oar, not a piece of clothing or a life-belt. Gottschalk had embarked on the *Cyclops*, going home on leave. The disappearance of the ship was eventually classed as one of the sea mysteries, like the *Marie Celeste*.

In a suburb of Rio de Janeiro, Villa Isabel, there was a spiritualist centre named Léon Denis. There are many such centres in Brazil. The Villa Isabel undertook to solve the mystery. At one of its sessions, a dead sailor of the *Cyclops* appeared through the appropriate medium and told the assembled adherents a story of what happened. What he said was duly taken down and the whole report found its way— nobody knows quite how—into the hands of the American Ambassador. Now these spiritualist séances in Brazil are not rated any higher than the *macumba* and *candomblé* fetishist meetings that abound in Brazil. But Ambassador Morgan sent the document he had received with a covering despatch to the State Department in Washington. His despatch was not acknowledged! Morgan wrote again asking for a reply. Rumour had it in diplomatic circles in Rio that he did get a reply. But it was merely one telling him to go on six months' leave "for the benefit of his health."

I think the explanation of the disappearance of the *Cyclops* is not that she was *spurlos versenkt* or else spirited away by some supernatural agency, but simply that she was overloaded and broke her back. She was an old ship; and it is, I believe, quite common for ships to suffer one or two cracks in the main hull girder after the lapse of twenty years or so.

As I had my own office in Rio de Janeiro, while the rest of the Embassy staff alternated between the Government's house in Petropolis and whatever house in Rio the Ambassador thought fit to rent for his stay there during the cooler months, it was a matter of congratulation for me to find that my colleagues were easy to get on with. The Embassy work was, in any case, almost entirely commercial, so that with rare exceptions all incoming papers came to me "for observations" or "for action." Indeed, Sir Ralph Paget, shortly after his arrival said to me: "If an ambassador here doesn't get through his work in a couple of hours a day, he doesn't know his job. The post is a commercial one, and you have the commercial work to do; so for you it is certainly a full-time job; but not for an ambassador." Nevertheless, there was always enough to occupy a Secretary like John Leche, or a Counsellor like Patrick Ramsay. I single them out because I found them particularly co-operative and competent. Indeed, Sir Patrick Ramsay, who was Chargé d'Affaires in Brazil in 1925 and 1926, went out of his way to be kind and helpful to me, not only when he was in Brazil, but when, later, he was Minister at Athens at a time when I was in the wilderness after incurring the displeasure of dictator Getúlio Vargas and having to leave Brazil at a moment's notice.

When I was Acting Consul-General at Rio de Janeiro I had become good friends with the Captain of *H.M.S. Amethyst*, Richard Webb, whose beat was the East Coast of South America. I had stayed with him at Portsmouth in 1912 when he was Captain of the War College, and had seen him in 1916 at the Admiralty when he was Head of the Trade Division there and we discussed contraband problems together. We kept up an occasional correspondence. After the 1914-18

War Admiral Sir Richard Webb was attached to the British High Commission at Constantinople. From there he wrote to me:

Constantinople,
30 Jan. 1919

My dear Hambloch,

It was indeed kind of you to send me your congratulations on this job.

It is an extremely interesting one in many ways, and quite suits me for the moment; the only fly in the ointment is that it is d—d hard, I find, to do No 2 again after having been No 1 for so long, as I was in the Trade Division at the Admiralty. However, it's very good discipline!

Our "Mission" is to make the Turk carry out the terms of the Armistice. You might just as well talk of making a cat produce puppies. Both are physical impossibilities. The Turk is an unspeakable brute, and the only thing he understands is the big stick—the bigger the better. And that is just what we haven't got: the blessed word "Demobilization" is all any one thinks about, and whereas they have millions of soldiers on the Western front to coerce the Hun, we have got about 2 men and a boy to perform a far more difficult job.

The crimes of the Turks are beyond words. I suppose that never in the history of the world have there been massacres on such a wholesale scale as those of the Greeks and Armenians. The way our men were treated in captivity, too, was appalling, and I do devoutly hope that the Peace Conference will make the Turk really suffer for his abominable sins.

The best of luck in your new capacity of Senior Commercial Secretary. I have no doubt you find the work hard but congenial.

All good wishes for 1919,

Yours ever,
Richard Webb.

THE LEVANT AND PALESTINE

A letter I received from Admiral Webb nearly two years later is perhaps even more interesting:—

> H.M.S. *Emperor of India*,
> 21. X. 20

My dear Hambloch,

Your letter of Sept. 8 has just reached me: ever so many thanks for it and for the kind congratulations it contains.

As you see by the above, I have left the Foreign Office's sheltering wing at Constantinople and have managed to get to sea once more—rather a business in these days of many Admirals and few sea-going jobs. But it's good to get to sea again, altho' I must admit that I had an extraordinarily interesting time at the High Commission, which I wouldn't willingly have missed for anything.

Now I am on my way to Malta, having finished a brief but very interesting cruise round the Levant: Smyrna, Cyprus, Beirut (now a nest of French officials), Haifa (alias Mount Carmel), Jaffa (change here for Jerusalem), and Alexandria, with a visit to Cairo chucked in.

I was specially glad to get a chance of seeing Jerusalem, Jericho, Bethlehem, Hebron, etc. and also of seeing how Samuel (with whom I stayed) was getting on. [Sir Herbert Samuel, later first Viscount.] He is doing extremely well, and the Arabs—who naturally were most bitter at first against his appointment—now seem to be settling down as quietly as might be hoped for. Syria is far from happy and Cilicia is a seething cauldron, nothing less.

In your remote and more or less tranquil political atmosphere I wonder how all the amazing complexities of Europe strike you. I suppose it is inevitable—the complexities I mean—and that it would have required supermen to bring about a satisfactory or lasting peace. But it's a d—d fine muddle, and he would be a brave man who would try and prophesy how it will all work out.

Your Report you kindly sent me is very interesting. It

recalls many old memories and I wish I could renew my acquaintance with the Station; but now that I am installed here, there doesn't seem much chance of that.

With all good wishes,

Yours ever,
Richard Webb.

A year before, Rio de Janeiro had the visit of one of the largest warships then afloat, *H.M.S. Renown* (32,500 tons). She had taken the Prince of Wales to Canada and from there brought to Rio Sir Ralph Paget, our first Ambassador to Brazil, who had accompanied the Prince to Canada.

When Paget landed at Rio on October 2, 1919, the British Embassy staff on the quay to meet him consisted of only two people: Ivone Kirkpatrick, Third Secretary, and myself. We were quite outnumbered by Brazilian officials from the Ministry of Foreign Affairs and the Brazilian Admiralty. The Brazilians made much of the occasion, of Sir Ralph, and of Lady Paget who followed him and to whose hospital work in Serbia during the early months of the First World War they paid well-deserved tributes. For Brazilian commentators the raising of the British Legation to the status of an Embassy was regarded as (I quote from a Brazilian review) "raising Brazil to the dignity of a Great Power."

The result of the multiplication of ambassadors, however, to the point when every head of a Mission was an ambassador— from Hungary to Haiti and, literally, from China to Peru— was that the compliment eventually lost all force.

"When everyone is somebodee,
Then no one's anybody."

That does not detract, necessarily, from the personal qualities of any of Sir Ralph Paget's successors. But does capacity really count today? Ivone Kirkpatrick, in a book he wrote after his retirement, did not fail to point out that, though the levelling of all heads of Mission was intended to ensure that in the eyes of the profane all ambassadors are equal, the FO mandarins marked out an Inner Circle in which a select number of ambassadors were more equal than others. Kirk-patrick himself was of that number. Having been First Secretary at our Embassy in Berlin he was able to act as personal trans-lator for Sir Nevile Henderson, who spoke not a word of German and whose own appointment during the Hitler régime, as he related in his *Failure of a Mission*, was as much a surprise to him as it was to everybody else.

One day Paget came to my house in Larangeiras, an old Portuguese building in Rio de Janeiro, the ground floor of which I had converted into an office. He often used to come and see me when he was in Rio. He had a wonderful steam car which, on its good days, could out-distance any other. Only his chauffeur, Miloye Milenkovitch, an Army mechanic whom he had attached to him when he left Serbia in 1914, could manage it. I, too, had an American car, a Willys-Knight, which I had bought from the widow of the assassinated President-maker of Brazil, Senator Pinheiro Machado.

"You and I will be in the black books of the British com-munity," Paget had said, "as we both have American cars."

"Quite possibly," I said. "But I have tried in vain to persuade two or three British firms, who say they would like to sell their cars in Brazil, to put the steering wheel on the left-hand side."

"Why don't they?" said Paget. "The rule of the road is on the right here, as it is in most countries."

"They tell me it is impossible; that it would mean re-designing the engine."

"Would it?"

"I don't know. I cannot argue with them on a technical matter. But Dunlop's representative here, whom I knew in Italy, says it's nonsense. He, too, drives an American car."

On this occasion, however, Paget had not come to talk about two things he liked: fast cars, and dogs; he always brought a dog with him. This time he mentioned a few official matters perfunctorily, and then fell silent.

Then suddenly he said: "I am leaving the Service."

"You can't be serious, sir," I exclaimed. "Unless it means that you don't like Brazil."

"I am afraid that is what people will say," said Paget. "But it is not so. I like Brazil and I like the post."

"Perhaps Lady Paget——" I began.

"No, she quite likes Brazil. The fact is I have been having a personal wrangle with some of my Foreign Office colleagues, so I am taking the opportunity of resigning. I have had my fill of diplomacy. I was born in an Embassy. My father was an ambassador; so was my grandfather—in Napoleon's time. In point of fact, I rather think that modern conditions have outgrown the old diplomatic set-up and the modern world is tired of all the useless flummery of cocked hats and gold-braided uniforms. Even when I was quite young in the Service and my father was ambassador in Rome I begged my mother to keep on our house near Florence, so that I could leave the Service and live there with our dogs and pictures and . . . and . . . But that is all past history. I shall be sorry to leave Brazil. But I want to get clear of diplomacy, and now is the time. The King [George V] will be very angry. But I can't help that. We were boys together. I expect they'll send Tilley to replace me. I remember you met him in London at the Government dinner to the FBI and its Brazilian delegation. I think you'll get along very well with him."

"I hope so," I said. "But is there no chance of your changing your mind?"

"No," said Paget. "I have already sent in my resignation officially."

I hated the thought of losing the best chief I ever served under, and far and away the most competent. Only Sir Beethom Whitehead, my chief at Belgrade at the outset of my career, was in the same class, for he, too, had that rare combination of kindness and competence, and the quick penetration that rejects all unessentials in any problem, so that the diplomatic démarches of the two men were courteously positive, and their despatches models of lucidity.

Paget was in England before the year (1920) was up, and wrote to me: "I am rushing about trying to find a family farm and settle down. . . . I often miss the sunshine and beauty of Rio intensely; but I am at the same time no less intensely glad to be out of official life. As I thought, your new Ambassador will be Sir John Tilley. I think he will do extremely well and be very efficient in all commercial matters. . . . When next you come over here don't fail to look us up, though it is scarcely likely you will find us still in London."

An engineer, Axel Hethey, was the moving spirit in a British attempt (unsuccessful) to set up an Anglo-Brazilian iron and steel industry in Brazil. We worked very hard on the scheme for over two years. I had had instructions from home to do all I could to help him, and we nearly pulled it off. Then at the last moment there were local intrigues, Canadian jealousies, American opposition, and a parochial-minded President who went back on his word. The site of the present Brazilian national steel industry at Volta Redonda is all part of the scheme that Hethey and I worked out together. Ah well, *nos, non nobis!* would have been Wileman's comment in his Brazilian review, if he had still been living.

As a young engineer Hethey had studied in Italy, while as a works manager he had had considerable experience in steel tube manufacture in England during the 1914-18 War. Stanley Baldwin was chairman of the group he worked for then, and I asked him to give me his impression of the man. I had never met him, but admired the classical turn of so many of his speeches. Baldwin, Hethey told me, had a remarkable faculty for "extraction and compression."

"What do you mean by that?" I asked him.

"Well, at a works meeting, for instance," said Hethey, "when technical and financial heads of departments would discuss production projects and other business Baldwin rarely put in a word. He let the discussion range freely. Then when conflicting views seemed to me to have become quite beyond reconciliation, Baldwin would take over. In very few words he would extract the pith of the differing arguments, disentangle them, weigh them up, and then say: 'I think we ought to decide thus . . .' and, whatever the decision, it would usually be accepted as the best solution."

One of the members of Hethey's small, but very influential, iron and steel syndicate came to Rio de Janeiro on business of his own: Lord Invernairn, chairman of William Beardmore & Co., which had been founded by his father. I introduced him to the Lage family, Brazilian shipowners, and one day I took him and his wife to the top of the Sugar Loaf by cable car. The cable had not long been inaugurated, and I asked him if he thought it was safe, for many local doubts had been expressed. He had a good look at the job and pronounced it to be a good piece of Brazilian engineering and quite safe—an opinion which time has confirmed. One evening at my house we were talking about family names, and I asked Lady Invernairn if her maiden name of Tullis was Scotch.

"It is really Roman," she said. "At least, that is what my family believe. They say it is a corruption of Tullius."

"And I am sure you must find pleasure in imagining a Ciceronian origin," I suggested.

I think she really did, for she gave me the impression of being imaginative. Lady Invernairn was dark and slenderly built. He was florid, sturdily built; a man in the late sixties, with piercing blue eyes. His manner was abrupt; hers very gentle. They seemed to be very fond of each other.

When the First World War was out of the way, many people seemed to behave as though it had never happened. International politics were discussed largely in terms of conferences —from Versailles to San Remo, Locarno, Spa, the Trianon, and Lausanne. The conference fever spread to other continents and covered a multitude of activities.

In Rio de Janeiro we had, in 1922, a Cotton Conference, and a Coal Conference; and in the following year an Americanist Conference. At each of them it was my job to represent our Government.

There were Missions, too. There was, for instance, a Montagu Mission, which came out to examine the Brazilian financial situation. I asked one of its members, Sir Charles Addis, a banker from the Far East, if they had been invited by the Brazilian Government, or had come out on their own account as representing financial interests in the City of London. He told me that "quite frankly" he did not know. The Mission achieved exactly nothing, and I don't think it even got much

nformation. To it the old music-hall ditty might aptly have
been applied:

"We all walked into the shop
To shelter from the rain;
The girl wouldn't show what we wanted to see,
So we all walked out again."

At a later date there was a Cutlers Mission from Sheffield.
This was headed by the Master Cutler, and one hoped to hear
something commercially illuminating. But the main theme,
indeed the sole theme, of all their speeches was not on trade
at all. It was a long elaboration of the fact that the Mission
had the backing of the British Government, "so much so that
each of us has been furnished with a Red Passport". The
Master Cutler would then explain at great length what an
honour (in his opinion) this was. Red passports were issued
only to couriers and other bearers of important despatches,
the accent being on the word Important. Then, as a kind of
afterthought, listeners were told that Sheffield cutlery was of
excellent quality. Which everybody in Brazil already knew.
Terms of trade and delivery were what they had wanted to
hear about.

"How many so-called business men join sponsored trade
missions simply for the ride, knowing that in any event half the
cost will be met by. . . ." That was not written in the 1920's,
but in 1966, and the concluding words of the remark are . . .
"the British National Export Council?" The paragraph
appeared in *The Times* under the heading: "Too many free
rides?" From the article quoted it appears that "the BNEC
had (by May, 1966) already paid out well over £100,000
on more than 100 missions . . . and has a liability to pay a
further £150,000". Where does this money come from that the
BNEC so lavishly spends? Does it add to the price of the goods
that are exported, presuming (a rash presumption!) that at
least some goods are exported as the direct result of the
pilgrimages of these missionaries? Or does the taxpayer pay?
Can missions replace "the commercial traveller"? Is the day of
the merchant banker and the merchant commission house past?

Cooks and head-waiters at times amused themselves in
concocting the menus for the banquets offered to commercial
and other missionaries of the 1920's. For instance, *Parfait d*
fois gras en Westminster, which seemed appropriate for a prid
of parliamentarians; or *Soufflé Rothschild*, which the Montagu
Mission may have found wanting in tact.

The most ingenious effort, however, was I think made by
the staff of the Adelphi Hotel in Liverpool, who concocted a
menu "in Celebration of the Signing of the Peace, 1919."
The Brazilian guests of the FBI were staying at the Adelph
Hotel, and Dr Pandiá Calôgeras, fresh from the Versaille
Conference, presided at the banquet. It was held on July 19
and he specially marked the date as being historical when he
signed my menu, which, I think, is worth giving in full. I
ran thus:

Diablotins de la Marne
Cantaloup Glacé Vimy

Consommé de Volaille à la Beatty

Dominion de sole Kitchener

Grenade de Filet Verdunoise
Petits Pois à l'Entente
Pommes à la Jellicoe

Crapouillauds* de l'Yser à la Haig
Salade Pershing

Albertines de Foie-Gras Lloyd George

Marmites de Pêche à la Foch
Joffrettes du Tigre

Délices de la Paix

Crapouillot (from *crapaud*, a toad) was a small trench mortar, so named from its
squat appearance, in the 1914-18 War, though it dates apparently from about
1880 as a trench weapon. A *crapouilloteur* was the artillery man who used the
weapon. I think the menu spelling must be wrong, though logical by derivation
—E.H.

Chapter XIII

*The Game of Power Politics — Another President-elect in London —
The Prince of Wales in Brazil — A Revolt — Some Parallelisms
— Fawcett legends and facts — Fascist nurseries — Toscanini takes
coffee — The Viper — My congé.*

D R EPITÁCIO PESSOA, the chief Brazilian representative
at the Versailles Peace Conference in 1919, was
unexpectedly elevated to the Presidency of the Brazilian
Republic. That meant that he made the usual round of visits
to European capitals. Arthur Knox Little, who had just
retired from his job as General Manager of the (British)
Leopoldina Railway in Rio de Janeiro, was then in London.
I saw him when he came to Brazil a short while afterwards,
and this is what he told me:—

"When we knew in the City that Epitácio was coming to
London, it was decided that the Lord Mayor should give him
a luncheon at the Mansion House. But on the morning of his
arrival I found that not a single person from the Government
would be at Victoria to meet him. So I dashed off to the Foreign
Office and got hold of Montgomery [Sir C. H. Montgomery
was then Marshal of the Ceremonies]. We went to the station
together. I told him I hoped King George would receive
Epitácio, just as the King of the Belgians had. Montgomery
told me this was out of the question: the King didn't receive
Presidents-elect. You know, this protocol business is very
silly."

"The trouble is," I reminded Knox Little, "that Presidents-
elect do not always take office. Some rival shoots his way into
power."

"Oh, that may be so in some small Central American
Republics," said Knox Little airily. "But not in a country like
Brazil."

N

Dr Epitácio Pessoa was not received by the King, and the question did not crop up again for ten years, because the next two Presidents-elect did not come to Europe. But in June 1930, the man officially given out in Brazil to doubting voters as their newly-elected President was Júlio Prestes de Albuquerque, and London was to receive a visit from him. I do not know from what quarters pressure was put on the Foreign Office, but the authorities in London decided to give Júlio Prestes the full treatment, which included being received by the King. It was the year of the Macdonald ministry and Arthur Henderson was Foreign Secretary.

Their decision was an unfortunate one. They must have been singularly ill-informed by our Embassy in Rio about the political situation in Brazil. If ever there had been an occasion when strict adherence to the time-honoured protocol about Presidents-elect was imperative, this was it. Instead, a colossal fuss was made in getting a royal reception for a man commonly regarded in Brazil as a mere puppet in the hands of a clique of political intriguers. It was with dismay that, from afar, I watched our authorities treating as a powerful foreign potentate a man who might not—and in the event did not—take office at all.

The Prince of Wales was at Victoria in full uniform as Colonel-in-Chief of the Welsh Guards, and there were field-marshals, admirals, and other dignitaries all lined up on the regulation red carpet in company with Arthur Henderson in levée dress and a host of Brazilian officials. Guard of Honour, State landau, Household Cavalry, a banquet offered by the King—nothing was lacking. But less than three months later, the gentleman "whom the King delighted to honour" took ignominious refuge in the house of a British consul in Brazil and was never heard of again in Brazilian public life.

On October 24, 1930, three weeks before he was due to hand over the Presidency to his "elected" successor Júlio Prestes, the President of the Republic, Dr Washington Luiz, was ousted from office in circumstances which I have related in some detail elsewhere.*

---

*His Majesty the President.

Getulio Dornelles Vargas

The man who organized this *coup d'état* was Getúlio Dornelles
Vargas. There seems to have been something prophetic in the
curious name bestowed on him at his baptism. The *Gaetuli*
in North Africa are known to us in history as a tribe which
double-crossed Pompey, and then suddenly deserted King
Juba to join the ranks of a conquering Caesar. Getúlio Vargas
was a native of Rio Grande do Sul. I had known him personally
when I was Commercial Secretary to our Embassy and he was
Minister of Finance in the Cabinet of his friend (!) and
political protector, Dr Washington Luiz.

Short, dark, with a bird-like face and inclined to be plump,
Getúlio Vargas was the very opposite of the lean, long-legged
gaúcho, typical of his native State of Rio Grande do Sul. But
if he was too short in the leg, he was extremely long-headed
and long-sighted—a man who knew what he wanted and was
determined to get it. He had a large mouth and thin lips. His
public smile for photographers was notorious; but the tightly
closed mouth revealed the tenacity of the ruthless politician.
In wiliness not even the astutest Brazilian politician—and they
are very astute—could equal him. In conversation he could be
very affable; and he was a good listener; unlike most Brazilians,
who are good talkers. Whenever I went to see Getúlio Vargas
on Embassy business when he was Minister of Finance, he
would wave me to a chair and then sit on the sofa with his
little legs curled up on it. (The three-piece set was part of the
normal furniture of a minister's sanctum.) He would listen
carefully to what I had to say, ask a question or two, take the
memo I had prepared for him to study, and ask me to come
back in a day or two for his reply. The day came; he was
punctual; and I got my reply. Nothing could have been more
business-like, or, I may say, more unusual in Brazilian official
procedure in those days, when after having had to play the
part of the importunate widow one would be lucky to get any
reply at all.

Having seized the presidency, Getúlio Vargas remained in
power as dictator for fifteen years—from November 1930 to
October 1945. He was then ousted by the Army, but was
elected Senator and was later returned to power as elected

President in 1951. Four years later, he shot himself. But that is another story.

By the end of 1930 Getúlio Vargas was firmly established in his dictatorship, and in the Spring of the following year the Prince of Wales, accompanied by Prince George (of Kent), arrived at Rio de Janeiro in a British warship. After being entertained officially by the Brazilian Government, he prolonged his stay in Brazil unofficially.

The visit was in many ways a great success, Brazilians being scarcely less enthusiastic than the British community. It would have been a complete success, had the visit not been marred by persistent unpunctuality on the part of His Royal Highness —and this in a country in which *pontualidade inglêsa* has passed into the language as proverbial.

I wrote a number of articles in the Brazilian press for the occasion, as well as virtually the whole special issue of the *Anglo-Brazilian Chronicle*, a British publication printed in São Paulo. I insisted on having an authoritative article on Brazilian music in the issue. Various professors of music were suggested; but I rejected them. I decided that something quite fresh was wanted, so I sought out an unorthodox musician, Heitor Villa-Lobos. He was a 'cellist already becoming notable for his work in "fixing the modern Brazilian musical idiom". I found him, long-haired and dusty in a dusty school-room, rehearsing a string quartet. He explained that he was overwhelmed with work and projects, and put me on to his friend Mario de Andrade, then the leading critic and exponent of modern Brazilian music. He wrote a really first-rate, informative article on the subject. I mention it because I know of no other essay dealing so succinctly with this aspect of Brazilian musical development.

It was in São Paulo that I spent most of my time in those years, and as the chairman of the British Chamber of Commerce there, J. D. Evans, was a particular friend of mine, I ghosted his speech for him at the dinner given to the Prince of Wales by the Chamber. Stories had reached us of the unpunctualities at Rio. The Prince arrived one hour late for the dinner, but he could be and was very disarming, and everybody liked him. The photographers in São Paulo would not leave him in peace. This bothered him, and one day on the golfcourse he exploded. "Can't you send these chaps away?" he said to Evans. "What do they think I am—a bloody monkey?" Of course, his programme was over-crowded, but on the whole he took it with great good humour.

He found time one day to look in at the British Club at cocktail time. Having chatted and sipped a cocktail, he left. When, after accompanying him to his car, we returned to finish our drinks, one of the party seized a half-full cocktail glass, held it up for all of us to see, drank off the contents, wrapped the glass up in his handkerchief, put it in his pocket and proclaimed with great glee: "This I shall keep for ever: the glass from which the Prince drank!" Loyal enthusiasm could go no farther. Or could it? On the mantelpiece in the drawing room of a house I was visiting in São Paulo a few days later was a long white kid glove enclosed in a glass case.

"Whose glove is that?" I asked my hostess, an English lady.

"Mine," she said proudly.

"What is it doing there?"

"I wore it at the ball to the Prince of Wales, and I touched him with it."

"But you didn't dance with him," I said. "He danced with only two ladies, the wife of the Consul and the wife of the Chairman of the Chamber. And then he left."

"That's true," said the lady. "But as he was dancing with Mrs Evans I stretched out my arm and managed to touch his back with that glove on my hand. Now it is sacred."

At the Chamber dinner a note was passed along from Prince George to his brother, who, after reading it, smiled and showed it to Evans who was in the chair. He, too, smiled, and said to the Prince: "Can I let Hambloch see it?"

"Yes, but let me have it back," said the Prince. This was the pencilled message from Prince George to his brother: "The man on my left talks nothing but Portuguese. The man on my right insists on talking German to me. I'm having the hell of a time. How are you getting on?"

I handed the note back to the Prince of Wales, who carefully tore it into tiny shreds.

As to the ball I have mentioned, there was some heart-burning among the ladies because he had not stopped longer than for the two almost obligatory dances I have spoken of. He went off to see a film, a private view, in the cinema of the Martinelli building. I had often met Martinelli before. He told me he had started life as a butcher's boy in the interior of São Paulo. Twenty-five years later he had become a shipping magnate. Apart from his own curious residence in Rio, Martin-elli had put up an 18-storey building for flats and offices in São Paulo. For years, it was the only sky-scraper in Brazil. I knew many people who would never walk in its shadow. They were afraid it would tumble down.

It was not to be expected that the São Paulo *políticos* would sit down quietly after one of their men (Washington Liuz) had been ousted from the Federal presidency and another (Júlio Prestes) prevented from succeeding him. So in 1932, they staged a revolt—they called it a Constitutional Revolution: it is a well-worn banner. *The Times* correspondent, as it happened, lived not in Rio, but São Paulo, and, like all Britons up and down Brazil, had absorbed the local colour. Dr Getúlio Vargas, he had told readers of *The Times*, was "completely subservient to the will of subordinates. . . . These men are undoubtedly the dictators in Brazil, Dr Vargas being a convenient and presentable figurehead without a say in the affairs of the nation." Never was there a more glaring and stupid travesty of the truth. I personally have no reason to have tender feelings for Getúlio Vargas. But one must give the man his due. He was a dictator in every sense of the word. His was a One-Man show if ever there was one!

When I saw the text of this telegram to *The Times*—my friend, the Consul, showed me the draft—I decided to go to Rio. Which I managed to do with some difficulty. One was going from one hostile camp to another! In Rio I got a Brazilian friend of mine to introduce me to the Chief of Police, Colonel João Alberto, one of Getúlio Vargas's closest and most trusted friends. On his part the Chief of Police was on very good terms with my friend, José Maria dos Santos, whose influence as author and journalist was considerable. The upshot of our interview was that Colonel João Alberto promised I might send any telegrams or despatches I liked to London, uncensored. It was a great concession, and I made use of it.

Some two years later I received a visit from an Englishman, Gilbert Doe, who brought with him a copy of a book about Brazil published in England. Doe had been wounded in the First World War, amused himself exploring the interior of Brazil, and occasionally took tourists with him on these expeditions. He had made friends with the chiefs of several Indian tribes, and was able to move about freely in their zones. Doe had apparently taken a party including the author of the book that he showed me on one of these jaunts. He ridiculed the author's description of having gone in search of Fawcett, the explorer who disappeared, and was particularly incensed at having, as he said, been maligned in the book under the guise of a purely fictitious character invented by the author. He asked for my help in rectifying all this. Of course, I could do nothing, though I sympathized with him. All travel books about Brazil, I reminded him, have to be taken with large pinches of salt. Incidentally, I said, I had some cause of complaint myself about the book, but could do nothing.

"You were already up country with the author and the rest of your party, I believe, when the São Paulo revolt broke out," I said to Doe.

"Yes," he replied; "and none of the people we met could tell me what it was all about."

"But the author of the book knew," I said.

"In his book he certainly gives the impression that he knew all about it. But at the time he had only been in the country a few days; and that, for the first time. He romanced about his trip with me up-country; but he got his facts right about the revolt."

"You know that I got out of São Paulo in the middle of the revolt and went to Rio," I said.

199

"Yes, and I read your summing up of the whole situation. Why, of course, that's where our friend got his facts from! Some of it is almost a literal transcription of your article. Is that fair?" asked Doe.

"Well," I replied, "one usually acknowledges one's source. But great minds proverbially think alike, and this may be merely a case of parallelism."

Historical examples are not wanting. Here is one that affects Brazil. I take it from "English Anthology" published in 1929 by Professor Nuno Smith de Vasconcellos of the Pedro II College, Rio de Janeiro.

Manifesto by Dom Pedro II, Emperor of Brazil, to Abraham Lincoln, President of the United States, in 1864, during the War of Secession:	Manifesto by Woodrow Wilson, President of the United States, to the world, in 1917, during the first World War:
I speak on behalf of humanity and the neutrals of South America, whose industry and commerce are seriously affected by this most unaccountable war. . . .	I spoke on behalf of humanity and of the rights of all neutral nations, like our own, many of whose interests the war puts in constant jeopardy. . . .
It is inconceivable that the mighty State of which I am Emperor would play no part in that enterprise.	It is inconceivable that the people of the United States should play no part in that great enterprise.
No peace that does not include the Brazilian empire can keep the future safe against a renewal of this uncalled-for war. . . .	No covenant of co-operative peace that does not include the people of the New World can suffice to keep the future safe against war. . . .

The statesmen of the Confederate States assure me they have no desire to crush the United States of America.	The statesmen of both groups of nations have said . . . that it was no part of the purpose they had in mind to crush their antagonists.
There must be peace without victory. . . .	They imply, first of all, that it must be peace without victory. . . .
The foundation of peace is the equality of the States.	The equality of nations upon which peace must be founded . . . must be equality of rights.
Mankind is looking for freedom, and slave-holding States are fighting for freedom. . . .	Mankind is now looking for freedom of life, not for equipoise of power. . . .

Incidentally, nearer home, there is the case of Disraeli's "pompous funeral oration on the Duke of Wellington." Half of it was found to have been taken "word for word from a panegyric by Thiers on Marshal Gouvion de St Cyr." Greville tells us that Disraeli was "unmercifully pelted" for this "piece of folly and bad taste." But it does not seem to have stood in the way of his political career, possibly because both folly and bad taste are inseparable from politics.

About the unfortunate Colonel Fawcett and his disappearance in Brazil enough has been written to compile a Fawcett Saga. Indeed, so much has been written by so many intrepid adventurers who profess to have penetrated impenetrable jungle that the few ascertainable facts have become hidden in a jungle of verbiage. I do not propose to add to the jungle. There are, however, one or two simple facts which, I think, ought to be stated.

We must start with the fact that long before Fawcett ever thought of coming to Brazil, the interior of the country had been well explored not only by European travellers in the nineteenth century, but more particularly in the 1900's by Colonel Candido Rondon, an engineer in the Brazilian Army, by his companions and subordinates, and by geologists like Gonzaga de Campos and Euzebio de Oliveira, both of whom I knew well. Rondon was eventually promoted general and field marshal. He was born in Brazil, the son of a French father and an Indian mother. Technically his job was to install telegraph lines all over the interior of Brazil. In the course of this work he was in daily contact with Indians, and towards them he felt he had a civilizing mission. He dedicated his life to this work, which resulted in the creation of a special Federal Department "for the Protection of Indians."

Rondon was a sparse, yellow-skinned, sinewy man, who would listen to one with seemingly illimitable patience. His eyes had a far-away look. Whenever I met him I felt I was in the presence of an exceptional man. He lived to be ninety-two. It was said of him that "his telegraph wires brought peace" to the Indians, of whom, in his long career, he classified sixty-five tribes, whose individual customs he insisted must always be respected.

If I have dwelt at some length on Rondon, it is to emphasize that Fawcett started off entirely on the wrong foot by not consulting him or some of his assistants before embarking on his quest for "a forgotten city of a vanished civilization." If ever there was a man with a bee in his bonnet it was Fawcett. Moreover, his disposition was imperious and impatient, and, as I should gather from what I personally saw of him, he was very self-opinionated.

It was when Sir Ralph Paget was ambassador (1919–20) that Fawcett came on his first visit to Brazil. He stayed for several days at the Embassy, which was in an old Portuguese-built, colonial-style house on the slopes of the Santa Teresa hill, with a splendid view over the bay. Of this Fawcett painted several water-colour views and gave some of them to Sir Ralph. Lady Paget confirmed this to me, but could not tell me what had become of them when Sir Ralph died in the south of France in 1940. In 1924 Paget had a farm at Sittingborne, and Fawcett visited him there before setting out on the Brazilian expedition from which he never returned.

Colonel Fawcett's wife kept in constant touch with Lady Paget and would never believe that her husband had died in Brazil. At least she was convinced that he "lived", and that she had telepathic contact with him. This appears from a letter she wrote to Lady Paget in 1953, in which she refers to the Colonel as Puggy. Apparently husband and wife were fond of nicknames, for Colonel Fawcett referred to her as Cheeky. A lady with spiritualistic gifts, Miss Geraldine Cummins, wrote a book on "The Fate of Colonel Fawcett" in 1955, in which she relates receiving "scripts" from the dead Colonel, she being apparently an "extremely gifted automatic writer." Lady Paget sent me a press cutting about the book, and wrote (December 6, 1955): "I am enclosing you an article which will interest you, as you knew the man [Fawcett]; but just because we knew him, can you imagine that this story is true? He would never have let the two boys [his son Jack and their companion Raleigh Rimmel] go by themselves in search of the Lost City, knowing the terrible dangers they would go through. When next I see you perhaps you would give me back the article, as I collect any article written about Colonel Fawcett."

In 1951 some bones were discovered in the Brazilian forests. They were alleged with great confidence by many people to be those of Colonel Fawcett. Assis Chateaubriand, owner of a chain of newspapers in Brazil, had them packed up and brought them to England, confident that the Colonel's son, Brian, would "verify" them as being those of his father. The story would have made a magnificent journalistic scoop. It was a macabre affair. The box was opened. Several people were present. Mr Brian Fawcett, after careful measurements had been taken, was able to declare positively that the bones could not be those of his father. Bitterly disappointed, Assis Chateaubriand muttered to a Brazilian friend of mine (in Portuguese): "This damned Englishman has spoilt the whole show!" However, characteristically enough, Assis Chateaubriand there and then invited Mr Brian Fawcett to come to

Brazil, promising—a promise that he kept—to procure every facility for him to go over the known terrain of the Fawcett expedition, interviewing Indians and so forth. Mr Brian Fawcett wrote a book about all this on his return. Some years later, Assis Chateaubriand was appointed Brazilian Ambassador in London. The appointment had nothing to do with the Fawcett affair.

My own view, as I wrote in 1933, still is that a friendly Indian guide accompanied Colonel Fawcett up to the limit of his "territory." He would go no farther, because in the neighbouring "territory" were hostile Indians. In any case, like most animals and some humans, Indians respect each other's tribal territory and will not encroach. Brooking no obstacle, Fawcett went on and perished at the hands of a hostile tribe. Another plausible version is that Fawcett lost his temper, accused his Indian guide of cowardice and slapped his face. The Indian took his revenge by following Fawcett secretly and killed him.

It has, too, always been my opinion that there has been only one properly organized expedition to look for Fawcett. It was one headed by an experienced traveller, George M. Dyott, who read a paper before the Royal Geographic Society on April 22, 1929, called "The Search for Colonel Fawcett."

Nothing that has appeared since then has upset the essential points of the modest and perfectly plain statements contained in that paper. Gilbert Doe, to whom I showed my copy Dyott's account first rate. Doe happened to know personally Dyott's Indian guide, and in fact saw him after his return from Dyott's expedition.

I have a voluminous dossier on Fawcett, chiefly from Brazilian sources; but I have already come near to breaking my promise not to add to the jungle of words that make up "The Fawcett Saga," of most of which Baron von Münchhausen himself would have been proud. I will, however, add a personal note or two.

In April, 1953, Lady Paget sent me a letter she had received from Colonel Fawcett's widow, who wrote from Torquay.

Mrs Fawcett wrote: "I salute you, dear Lady Paget, as one of the outstanding Great Ladies of First World War fame, when you did such valuable work with your Ambulance. . . . Since I first met you at Warren House much water has flowed under the bridge. It was there that I met your friend Zahr Pritchard [a numerologist] and heard so much that interested me intensely. Strange to say, that same Zahr Pritchard met P.H.F. (Puggy) [Colonel Fawcett] and Jack [the son who went with him to Brazil] in the United States and they were fellow passengers on the same boat, bound for Rio and the South, the Lamport & Holt liner *Voltaire*, when Zahr discussed the whole matter of the Hebrew Science of Numbers, telling them that all of our own family should at once (!) change our names to the names we *ought* to have had at birth, in order to ensure success in our undertakings! He said my name NINA was quite wrong, for the I in Nina denoted Sacrifice, and he worked out that I should have been called RULOR. Well, as you must admit, that would have brought a lot of—what can I call it?—sneering laughter in its train; not that *that* matters, for I follow a very wise bit of advice my beloved *first* husband, Capt. H. C. Prichard, 48th Northamptons, gave me in the valuable short months he was given to me before he 'passed on'—(we were married on June 29th, 1897) but he died *suddenly* on his 42nd birthday, 22 Nov. 1897:

> Do the work that's nearest,
> Though it's hard at whiles,
> Helping, when you meet them,
> Lame dogs over stiles.

Well, H. C. Pakoys [Prichard] used to say: 'You and Fawcett are meant for one another—I am only "an interloper." ' (My God! the best human character I have ever met! and a true Christian in every sense of the word!) and one other thing he said to me was:

> Follow the dictates of your own heart,
> And snap your fingers at the world.

Well, somehow I feel *very strongly* that I am to tell *you* all this. Somehow. How? It is not for me to know; but you *may* know. I get these *impulses*; and speak openly and frankly, as my Invisible Guides prompt me, and when I have said or written that which I am *meant* to say, I am 'shut off', as if the shutter of a camera closed when the photograph was taken!

"I came here to Torquay, not only because of its beauty, but because our Puggy [Colonel Fawcett] was born here, and it was here and at Teignmouth where he spent most of his time — from 5 years old, down on the beaches, watching, and chatting to boatmen, fisher folk, and men of that ilk, and where he cultivated his love of the Sea and all sorts of craft, the result bearing fruit in the lovely yachts he built *with his own hands;* first the *Nina,* 18 ft centre-board sloop; and later *My Sweetheart* (Menãchi, in Tamil), a 60 ton schooner capable of doing the trip to the Andaman Islands, and with which he carried off the First Prize, against the Admiral of the East Indian Squadron, who, when at Bombay, had 'swept the board' with his lovely Cowes-built racing yacht. Sir William Kemsday was the Admiral, and that must have been at the end of last century. . . .

"Well, dear Lady Paget, here I am, very happy indeed and plenty to do. . . I commuted half my pension to pay for P.H.F's [Colonel Fawcett's] last Expedition. However, the Good God helps those *who help themselves,* and I certainly do *that* to the very limit of my physical capacity. But now I must close (Friday, 17th April—6 p.m.!)

Very sincerely Yours,

Nina A. Fawcett

otherwise RULOR!"

"I have come to the conclusion," commented Lady Paget in a letter to me (April 23, 1953), "that if Mrs Fawcett called her husband Puggy, it was quite in order for him to call her Cheeky. I never heard two more inappropriate nicknames! I shall immensely look forward to seeing you and Mrs Hambloch as soon as the weather improves, when we can sit in the garden and talk our heads off! We will discuss the Fawcett book, as well as many other subjects, when you come here."

In the year before the São Paulo revolt of 1932, Gilbert Last, Secretary of the British Chamber of Commerce in São Paulo, asked me to collaborate with him in compiling a Brazilian *Who's Who*. Nothing of the kind existed. The disturbances of 1932 interrupted the work, but eventually we did manage to produce it. We engaged scouts to go out with printed questionnaires to be filled in by eligible people. They received a fee for every filled-in sheet, provided we accepted it. We found some of the scouts to be plausible forgers. Others interviewed people we could not possibly include in the *Who's Who*. For instance, Josephine Baker had come to Brazil, and one of our scouts, a Brazilian, was very indignant at my refusing to accept her name and activities for inclusion in the book.

"Talented though the lady is," I explained to him, "she does not belong to Brazil; nor is she a Brazilian. She is merely here like any other visiting foreign artist."

"But she is the Venus of Ebony!" was his excited reply.

Josephine Baker had only a *succès d'estime* in Brazil. The reason was, I think, that there are so many native ebony Venuses on and off the stage.

São Paulo, with its exuberant Italian atmosphere in those days, was a more exciting place to live in than Rio de Janeiro, where the tradition was more stolidly Portuguese. The Italian *Giovanezza* centre in São Paulo was well housed, well managed, and well frequented. It was supported by Mussolini when he came to power, but it already existed, and as a youth movement its activities were many and varied. It had its own orchestra under the direction of a young Italian professor of music, Callia, of whom my wife and I saw a good deal, for he came to our house frequently and we made much music together. We became great friends of him, his wife and his four stalwart sons, two of whom had been born in Brazil. I have already given the opinion of Martinelli, an Italian business man, on Mussolini. One day I asked Callia what he, as an artist, thought of the *duce*.

"I didn't leave Italy because of Mussolini," he replied gaily. "I came to Brazil because I felt I could get on quicker in my profession here than in Italy. And so it turned out. After only two years here, I could afford to bring out my wife and our two boys. I am earning much more than I could earn in Italy."

"I expect yours is an overcrowded profession in Italy," I said. "But you haven't answered my question. What is your opinion of Mussolini?"

"I know nothing about politics," said Callia. "As far as I can judge, he has got rid of much of the muddle we lived in."

"Tell Mr Hambloch about your score," interposed his wife.

"Yes, that is certainly worth relating," said Callia. "I had composed a symphony and sent it to Ricordi, the music publishers in Milan. Of course, they are such big people that I didn't expect an immediate reply from them. However, eventually I wrote them a reminder, saying I hoped they would accept and publish. I got no reply. I wrote twice again, asking them to return me my score. No reply! One day, my wife said to me: 'Why don't you write to Mussolini?' I hesitated, but eventually I did. Within a fortnight I got a reply from one of his secretaries saying my letter would be looked into. Then, would you believe it, at the end of another fortnight Ricordi sent me back my score, with the usual letter of regrets that one expects from publishers."

"Why don't you get your *Giovanezza* orchestra here to perform your symphony?"

"Oh, it's too difficult for them now. Perhaps one day. . . "

Callia was much excited because Toscanini was coming to São Paulo to conduct the orchestra at the Municipal Theatre, and it was hoped he would look in at the *Giovanezza* centre. It may be recalled that Toscanini had left Italy because he refused to open his concerts with the Fascist hymn.

As bad luck would have it, on the very day that Toscanini was to visit the Italian Youth Centre Callia was recovering from a bad bout of influenza and could not leave his house. I had gone to pay him a visit on that day. I found him rather pale and very disconsolate in an armchair. Presently the bell rang and his wife came in accompanied by a white-haired man whose features one at once recognized.

"Oh, maestro, maestro!" cried Callia, rising with difficulty from his chair. "What an honour!"

"Not at all," replied Toscanini with a kindly smile as he pushed Callia gently back into his chair. "They told me at the Centre that you were ill, so I wanted to see who had been training the little orchestra." Here was a celebrity not unbending, but perfectly natural.

Introductions followed, but I took my leave, in order to leave them to talk freely in Italian on their own. Madame Callia, usually an exceptionally calm and collected person, was obviously a little flustered at this unexpected visit. She was offering "wine, or some other refreshment," but Toscanini replied: "No, no; nothing of that. Just a cup of coffee *a nostro modo*, you know!" Arturo Toscanini wanted a real taste of home!

During my free-lance years in Brazil I came into even closer contact than before with men who confess that they are "political addicts." As a matter of fact, the addiction is universal among educated Brazilians. It is taken for granted that one likes talking politics. When the air was thick with cigarette smoke in my study at São Paulo and the clock showed that midnight was being left far behind, my thoughts would go back to my young days in Zurich and the late sessions with Russian students on the stairs of Frau Dr Liebetanz's pension. Then the talk had been indeterminate and of a Slav vagueness; but my Brazilian friends were grown men, lawyers, writers, and doctors, for doctors in Brazil take to politics as other men do to a hobby, and everything was definite, of a Latin incisiveness, and, to my mind, over-simplified. Besides merely local politics, the topic would usually be a comparison between parliamentary and presidential systems of government. One man would pull down from my shelves Hallam's *Constitutional History of England*, and another would consult Bryce on the American Constitution, while my friend José Maria dos Santos

209

O

would loll back smoking his pungent "straw" cigarettes and quote Montesquieu and other French authorities from memory.

José Maria dos Santos had lived in Paris for many years and married the daughter of a French senator. He was a living personification of the fundamental racial mixture in Brazil: Indian-Portuguese-African. He was an imposing figure: tall and spare. He had a broad forehead, eyes of an indefinable green-grey, well formed lips, and the wide mouth of a born orator. As a young officer he had fought in the famous Canudos campaign in the north-east scrubland of Brazil. Widely read and speaking very good French, he was a brilliant journalist and author. Dishonest politicians feared what he wrote, as much as honest men admired it. He had a wonderful command of the Portuguese language. I translated into English one of his books—on Brazilian Polity, and we saw a great deal of each other. I mention all this because it explains to some extent how it came about that, three years later (in 1935), my residence in Brazil was abruptly terminated.

It is a golden rule that a foreigner residing in a foreign country should never become associated with, much less take part in, local politics. It is a rule which I have always obeyed. But there is no rule that I know of against writing about the politics of a country. It is, however, sometimes dangerous when the local régime is one of dictatorship.

A retired Appeal Court Judge, Perestrello de Carvalhosa, was a friend of mine and frequently joined our little cigarette-smoking debating club in my study at São Paulo. His work as legal adviser to European owners of vast estates in Mato Grosso took him frequently to that State, and on his travels he would send me news about what he used to call "the latest Fawcett fairy tale". He kept up the correspondence after I had left Brazil. "These constant flights are beginning to tire me too much," he wrote to me from Corumbá (Mato Grosso) in September, 1938. "Here I am once again in Mato Grosso. I sent you a book when I passed through São Paulo [he was always sending me books]. It will help you write the other book I have always insisted you *must* write—the one on the city of

Rio de Janeiro, its history and, above all, its romance. You
must find time to do it. In the meantime, you will be amused
to learn that a Brazilian travesty of Hobbes's *Leviathan* is now
being actively propagated by Gê-Gê [Getúlio Vargas]. It is
called 'The New Order!'

"The Fawcett fairy tale grows and grows. It is now fortified
by a photograph of some local Indians, with an Indian woman
carrying in her arms a white child—'a grandson of Fawcett's'.
I suppose that because, as we know, the story of a much
photographed albino Indian child being Fawcett's was scotched
long ago, it has now become necessary that Fawcett's son
should have survived (where?) and likewise produced a child!
On the spot where the Colonel [Fawcett] was last seen a
Protestant mission has been set up under a Mr Young. . . ."

Carvalhosa speaks of "the other book" because the book I
had already written, *His Majesty the President*, had been done
very largely at his insistent prompting. His experience of the
European interests he represented in Mato Grosso had convinced him that people in Great Britain, as well as other countries, had no real notion of Brazilian political development.
They were only too ready to swallow what writers of sensation
told them from time to time. There had been worthwhile books
by people like Lilian Elliott and W. H. Koebel, but they had
covered only the material side of Brazil's development. No
modern writer had discussed the Brazilian from the Aristo-
telian standpoint as "a political animal." I could do it and
should do it, he insisted.

That had been the line of Carvalhosa's argument. Eventually
I yielded to it. Whenever my enthusiasm flagged, I would find
José Maria dos Santos at one elbow and Carvalhosa at the
other—they were inseparable friends—urging me on. One day
I finished the job and sent it home. I called it *His Majesty the
President*. It was published in London and, later, in New York.
But six or seven months were to elapse before that, during
which I had been invited to be Secretary of the British Chamber
of Commerce that I founded in Rio twenty years earlier. I
had been appointed *The Times* correspondent too. So my wife
and I left São Paulo, took a flat on the Gloria hill in Rio de

Janeiro and settled down to what promised to be a new and pleasant routine. But the promise was illusory.

A shoe-shine in Brazil was an armchair affair. In Rio, in a narrow arcade under the Avenida Hôtel in the centre of the town there was a row of these chairs on a platform. The operator sat on a low stool in front of his customer. One morning in October, 1935, on my way to the office, I climbed into one of the armchairs, placed my feet on the rests, and began thinking of the day's work ahead of me. My shoe operator had put the inevitable lottery ticket on my knee, saying nothing. It was the traditional invitation to buy; nothing was said, and no offence was taken if one didn't buy. On the walls of the arcade anything that took the fancy of the shoe-shiners could be pinned up. There was usually a varied collection of highly coloured advertisements: travel, theatre, a coming lottery, the latest popular song—anything. But on that morning, as my shoe-shiner operated and I had begun thinking vaguely of the subject for an article to be put in the next issue of our *Chamber of Commerce Bulletin*, I became aware that the wall opposite me was lined not with the usual variety of advertisements, but with a dozen sheets all showing the same picture—something in yellow, with bits of green and white print round it. I was too far away to decipher anything; but as I got up and paid I asked the shoe-shiner what it was all about.

"I've no idea," he told me. "All I know is that a group of university students came along very early this morning and asked us to take down all other placards and put up these things in their place. I can't read or write, so I don't know what is on them."

While he was talking I went up close to read the yellow placards.

"What is it all about?" asked the shoe-shiner.

"It looks as though it's about *me*," I said slowly, for I felt a trifle dizzy. "But I'm afraid I cannot explain."

I moved out of the shady arcade and walked slowly along the Avenida towards the offices of the Chamber. I thought the sunlight must be blinding me. But no. Festooned round the lamp-posts in the middle of the road, from one end of the

Avenida to the other, were the same coloured placards, but in much larger size. They were, as I was to discover later, reproductions of the cover of a Penguin-sized book, the title of which in bold print was: *Esmagando a Víbora!* (Crushing the Viper!). Other wording informed the reader that "His Magesty (*sic*) the President" was an "Affront to Brazil". The printing was in white, black, and green. The centre-piece was a herculean figure coloured yellow. The right fist was clenched. In his left hand, held in a crushing grip, was a large green serpent. The body of the reptile formed the £ sign, the tail of which was firmly held down under the right foot of this, evidently, Brazilian Hercules.

The booklet, on sale for a few milréis in all kiosks, contained a distorted and jumbled collection of Portuguese-translated extracts, all out of context, from my book *His Majesty the President*. The vituperative introductory notes were of an hostility to make recent (1966) criticism of a Lope de Vega play in English sound, by comparison, like a paean of praise. At the end of the booklet was a photograph of myself, over which were the words: *The Viper!* Underneath were my name and the words: *Brazilians! Let us Crush him!*

Why the £ sign as a reptile on the cover? The introduction to the booklet gave the clue. Its first sentence ran: "Foreign bankers aspire to transform the Brazilian Fatherland into a Protectorate of international usury, and for this purpose they attempt, through their hosts of exchange speculators, to exploit the Brazilian economy, destroy our national patrimony, and annihilate the liberty of all Brazilians." In this lengthy introduction I was stigmatized as the representative of "the libellous insolence of British capitalism."

It was only some days later that my Brazilian friends managed to discover whence all this pseudo-nationalist attack originated. It was from Rome. Mussolini had sent to his partisans in Brazil (he did not lack them during the Abyssinian campaign, the President of the Republic, Getúlio Vargas, being the most prominent) £1,000 for them "to discredit some prominent Englishman in Brazil." I was "prominent" enough for that purpose, and had no official standing. Brazilian

Fascists called themselves Integralists, wore green shirts, and saluted each other by raising an arm and shouting *Anaué*—an Indian war cry.

When I arrived at my office after my shoe-shine my very charming and highly efficient secretary, Ruby Peel, greeted me by saying: "I suppose you have seen all the placards, or did you come by car?"

"No," I said, "I ran the gauntlet on foot."

"What are you going to do?" she asked.

"The first thing I must do is telephone to my wife not to come to town. We may be in for trouble. This looks to me like the beginning of an organized campaign of violence."

"But your book already had some good notices here," said Miss Peel.

"Yes," I said, "but Gertsch, the Swiss Minister, told me the other day to be on the look-out for trouble and hinted it might come from Italy. I must be in bad odour with some of Mussolini's friends here."

I had known Gertsch ever since I first came to Brazil twenty-five years earlier. He was then a Swiss merchant. A few days before the events I am relating, we had met on the quay, each of us waiting to greet friends arriving from Europe.

"Ah," said Gertsch, coming up to me. "I see you have written a book."

"Yes," I said. " I believe it is on sale here already."

"You will have trouble," he said with some emphasis, waving a finger at me.

"Do you mean because I have said in my book a few things that wanted saying? Well, I have only told the truth."

"Dat is the trouble, my friend," said Gertsch smiling. "It is very dangerous to tell the truth. Ah, now the gangway is down, so I leave you. But remember, you will have trouble— and from Rome!"

That had been our conversation, and I was still thinking it over when the manager of the Royal Mail Lines came in, closed the door behind him, leant against it, and said dramatically: "Now you've done it!"

"Done what?" I asked.

"The students are going to smash our window," he said. "They are going to smash *all* the windows of *all* the British firms in Rio."

The Chamber of Commerce offices were on the first floor of the Royal Mail building in the Avenida. On the ground floor the Royal Mail had a large plate-glass window with a ship model in it.

"How do you know?" I asked.

"We have had a visit from a police detective. The Ministry of Justice is sending two plain-clothes police to be on the premises of every British firm. The students are organizing a mass demonstration against you. It is to be on the steps of the Municipal Theatre."

"Demonstrations are quite common occurrences," I said.

"Maybe. But after the speeches they are going to march through the town throwing bricks at every British office. Where they can, they will invade the premises and throw everything into the street. That's what you've done."

"Look here," I replied, much nettled, "I will save your precious plate-glass window by going home right away. You can tell your police friends where they can find me, and the students will probably leave you in peace."

The student meeting was held, as planned, on the steps of the Municipal Theatre. But there was no march, and no depredation of the premises of British firms. Why nothing happened I learnt many days later from my friend Perestrello Carvalhosa, the judge. To him one might have applied the epithet given to Melbourne's secretary, Young, who, Greville tells us in his diary, was called "Ubiquity Young", because "he knows many people, many places, and many things".

The placards were removed from the lamp-posts, and by the evening of this, for me eventful, day, all was calm outwardly. At night the door of my flat was smeared with the Fascist sign, and anonymous threats of violence and murder were pushed through our letter box or telephoned to me.

The Council of our Chamber agreed that it might be well if I went to São Paulo for a few days, where my wife and I still had our house. Within a few hours of our arrival in São Paulo,

Dr Octaviano Alves Lima, a leading figure in São Paulo political and social life, invited us to go and stay a few days at his farm in Campinas "until this silly storm has blown over," as he put it. I accepted his invitation, and we were glad of the restful peace of his well-organized coffee estate for a few days.

While we were there, a note had been received at our flat in Rio and was sent on to our house in São Paulo. It was an official request for me to call and see the Federal Minister of Justice, Dr Vicente Rao. I had never met Rao personally, but knew several friends of his. He was born in São Paulo of Italian parents, and when Getúlio Vargas found it prudent to give a constitutional wrapping to his dictatorship, he formed a new Cabinet and made Rao his Minister of Justice. Rao was an extremely able lawyer, too "Brazilian" in the eyes of many of the numerous Italian colony in São Paulo to be popular among them. I sensed at once that he would have got wind of the Italian instigation of the campaign against me, though that did not reassure me. However, I returned from Campinas to São Paulo, where my Brazilian friends were of opinion that it would be rash for me to go back to Rio de Janeiro for the express purpose, as they put it, of "walking into the lion's den." It is not uncommon for people deemed inconvenient by dictators to disappear. "In any case," added my friends, "if Rao really wants to get hold of you, he can always have you arrested." A cheerless prospect. But it was not many days before I received another sort of invitation, which cancelled out Rao's. It was an intimation to leave Brazil.

However, to go back a bit. While I was "resting" at Campinas, Carvalhosa had called on a friend of his at the Brazilian Ministry of Foreign Affairs and asked him confidentially if he knew why the students' threatened violence against British firms had not taken place. He was advised to go and see João Neves da Fontoura.

Dr João Neves da Fontoura was then a man of about forty-five. He was a graduate of Law in the university of Rio Grande do Sul, his native State. As a young student he and Getúlio Vargas had been "liberal" propagandists. But whereas Getúlio had veered off to Fascist doctrines, João Neves had remained true to his liberal principles. He had even fought with the rebels in the 1932 revolt, and then, fearing to walk into the lion's den when the affair was over, had gone into exile. After a while he had come back, and was not molested. He was held in the highest esteem not only by liberal thinkers but also by Brazilian students.

This is the account of what happened when Carvalhosa called on João Neves. I tell it in the latter's own words, as passed on to me by Carvalhosa.

"A deputation of students—about ten—came to see me a few days ago. They told me about their having placarded the town and their intention to wreck the offices of British firms here in Rio as a gesture of reprisal against what your friend Ernest Hambloch has written in his book *His Majesty the President*. They invited me to come and speak at the mass meeting they were to hold on the steps of the Municipal Theatre. They know my liberal views. Everybody knows them. If I would speak, they said, they would be able to get other prominent men to speak too.

" 'What do you want me to speak about?' I asked them.

" 'About the book this Englishman has written,' they cried, putting the booklet *Esmagando a Víbora* into my hands. I handed it back to them. Then I looked round the room and said: 'What you have handed to me is a *galimatias* of distortion. How many of you ten students have read the book itself, the original —Hambloch's book?' There was no reply.

" 'Now listen,' I told them. 'I *have* read the book. There is nothing in it to justify all this tumult that you are getting up: nothing. And for that reason I am certainly not prepared to speak at your meeting. Moreover, I advise you to give up your idea of doing violence to British firms.' They went away crestfallen. They were really very silly. But one does a lot of silly things when one is a student."

The meeting on the steps of the Municipal Theatre turned out to be a damp squib. But the Brazilian dictator had reasons of his own—to use a schoolboy expression—for sucking up to

Mussolini; and I was an easy victim. Perhaps it gave some satisfaction to the Italian dictator to see an insignificant person like myself humiliated at a time when public opinion in Great Britain condemned his Abyssinian adventure, and to know that the Brazilian dictator was on his side.

Ten years later (in 1946) when Getúlio Vargas had been ousted from power, João Neves da Fontoura was the new President's (Gaspar Dutra) Minister of Foreign Affairs, and I received a message from them both to say I might return to Brazil whenever I liked.

INDEX